OLD PROVINCE TALES
ARCHIBALD MACMECHAN

Books by Archibald MacMechan

The Porter of Bagdad
The Life of a Little College
The Winning of Popular Government
Sagas of the Sea
Head-Waters of Canadian Literature

Edited
Carlyle, Sartor Resartus
        Heroes and Hero-Worship
                    Essay on Burns
Nova Scotia Archives II. and III.
Tennyson, Select Poems

OLD PROVINCE TALES

by Archibald MacMechan

Decorations by
J. E. H. Macdonald, A. R. C. A.

McClelland & Stewart
Publishers   -   Toronto

Copyright, Canada, 1924,
by McClelland & Stewart, Limited, Toronto.

Printed in Canada.

TO

JEAN, GRACE, EDITH

THREE DAUGHTERS OF THE OLD PROVINCE

THESE ILLUSTRATIONS OF ITS HISTORY

ARE AFFECTIONATELY DEDICATED

BY

THEIR AUTHOR

Contents

OLD PROVINCE TALES

CONTENTS

Preface

THESE true tales are drawn from the romantic past of Nova Scotia, and have been studied from authentic documents. In each case, the reader is referred to the original authority. Pains have been taken to verify details. For example, in preparing the narrative of the loss of the *Tribune,* I went along the Thrum Cap shoals in a tug, and had soundings taken.

The various episodes here gathered together illustrate the history of Nova Scotia. They are arranged in order of their occurrence.

The escape of the three French gentlemen from Quebec in 1725 shows how ancient is the practice of sending family black sheep to the colonies. Their experience of Indian treachery, their flight from the fear of Indian vengeance open the chapter of the white man's relations with the red. Indian warfare was the nightmare of early settlers in America.

11

The experience of Marie Payzant and her family is the fullest recorded in any Canadian document telling of white captives' life among the savages. Witherspoon's narrative is based on a transcript of his journal kept during his imprisonment at Miramichi and Quebec; it was written in tobacco juice when ink failed. Both Nova Scotians were in Quebec when it fell in 1759. Fragments of their stories have been handed down, but many other early settlers suffered as they did, and died, and left no sign.

William Greenwood's efforts to run with the hare and hunt with the hounds reveal aspects of the American Revolutionary War not generally known. A natural pendant to the non-combatant's hardships is the tale of Tonge's two spirited fights in the coastal waters of Cape Breton.

Many a tall ship has left her bones along the iron coast of Nova Scotia. Many a wreck, and many a rescue are briefly noted in the annals of the province. The tragedy of the *Tribune* impressed the community by its completeness, and by the fact that young officers in the Duke of Kent's regiment lost their lives by going to the as-

sistance of the stranded frigate. Few
more determined efforts to save life at all
hazards to the rescuer are on record than
the two trips of 'Joe Cracker' to the half-
submerged masts of the *Tribune*. Little
more than a child himself, he saved the
lives of two men; and his heroic example
shamed the men of the Cove into saving
the six survivors. His exploit ranks with
Grace Darling's; and he had no one to help
him.

How the *Shannon* fought the *Chesapeake* is an oft-told tale; but the part
which the good old city of Halifax had in
it is not so well known.

The saga of the blood-stained *Saladin,*
like the murders on board the *Lennie* and
the *Caswell,* reminds the landsman how
often deeds of violence were done on the
high seas. Nova Scotians remember the
Saladin, for ballads made about the murders are still extant. One is to be found
in MacOdrum's MS collection of Nova
Scotia ballads preserved in Dalhousie College. In the case of both the *Saladin*
and *Lennie,* Nemesis followed close on the
heels of crime. Stevensonian touches occur in the tale of the *Saladin.* Like Long

John Silver, the villain has a wooden leg.
Like the murderous captain in *Kidnapped,*
Fielding reprobated 'Sandy's' cursing and
swearing. The murderers taking their
Bible oath 'to be brotherly together' re-
sembles the incident of the conscience-
stricken homicides repeating the Lord's
Prayer in unison on the deck of the *Flying
Scud.* The ring-leader in the murders on
board the *Caswell* made one sailor kneel
in the blood of the slain captain and swear
fealty to the mutineers. The Bible on
which Captain Fielding swore his red-
handed accomplices is preserved in Dalhousie College, the grimmest relic, save
one, of this sordid tragedy.

Privateering in Nova Scotia began in
1756, when the hundred-ton schooner
Lawrence sailed to the southward on a
six months cruise against the enemies of
George the Second. Part of her adventures are related in *The Log of a Halifax
Privateer, Nova Scotia Chap-books, No.
6.* In three great wars, Nova Scotia
privateers scoured the seas, made prizes,
fought and won, or fought and lost. Such
battles as the action between *Observer* and
the *Jack,* and between the tiny *Revenge*

and three 'rebel' privateers are known only in outline, and must be typical of many a sea-duel recorded briefly in long lost log-books. Godfrey's exploits in the *Rover* show the mettle of the old provincial sea-faring men. His victory over his four opponents is a classic, and wins the admiration of professional sailors for his cool courage, discipline and seamanship.

Heroism is not confined to action under stress of war. The courage, skill, endurance and resource of Nova Scotia's merchant sailors are hard to parallel. Before the era of railways, Nova Scotia was in reality an island; communication with the outer world, and between different parts of the province was by sea. These conditions bred a sea-faring race. Whole families followed the sea from generation to generation. Nova Scotia ship-masters took their wives and families with them on voyages round the world. Children were born on ship-board, literally in the midst of storms. The deeds of Cook and Coward, of the two Churchills herein recorded are typical. Chance has preserved their stories; but many others just as splendid have been lost for lack of a chronicler.

2

'Rendering assistance' is instinctive and habitual with sailors, by land as well as by sea. To those practical seamen, who opened freely to me their stores of professional knowledge and who gave me the benefit of their friendly criticism my grateful thanks are due; and especially to Captain W. G. S. de Carteret, Captain Fred Ladd, Captain Charles Doty, Captain H. St. G. Lindsay, Captain Neil Hall and Mr. Adams MacDougall. Without their assistance, my 'navigation' must have been very faulty. My thanks are also due to Mr. J. Murray Lawson, the historian of Yarmouth, for much personal aid. His records of Yarmouth shipping and the files of his paper *The Yarmouth Herald* are veritable store-houses of information.

I

The Slaying of Aeneas

I

The Slaying of Aeneas

N the 9th of December, 1725, the monotony of garrison life at Annapolis Royal was broken by an unusual event. Early that morning a shivering sentry in his watch-coat on the snowy ramparts of Fort Anne had observed a black speck far down the Basin creeping along the northern shore. When it could be clearly made out as a canoe with three figures in it coming up with the tide, he reported the occurrence to his sergeant. The canoe made for the Queen's wharf, directly under the guns of the fort, and the sergeant carried the news to the Hon. John Doucett, the lieutenant-governor, major of Philips's Regiment of Foot. It was soon ascertained that the strangers could speak only French, that they were not Acadians, and that by their own account they had travelled all the way from Quebec. Other rumors flew about, that they had killed Indians and were flying from savage vengeance. All the circumstances were so suspicious that the governor ordered Sergeant Danielson to take a file of men, arrest the strangers, and lodge them in the guardroom of Fort Anne. The three ragged, famished scarecrows offered no objection to their arrest. They even seemed to welcome it. They were stiff with paddling, pinched with cold, and weak with hunger. They were barely able to walk, and could have made no effectual resistance even had they desired to use the arms they carried.

As soon as possible, the governor convened a meeting of the Council in his house within the walls near the old Bastion de Bourgogne. Only Mr. Adams, the senior member, Mr. Skene, the surgeon, and Mr. Shirreff, the secretary, were available. Major Armstrong was in England on his private affairs, and Captain Mascarene was also absent on leave, arranging a treaty with the Indians at Boston. As soon as the members had taken their places round the board in the order of precedence, Mr. Adams at the right hand of the governor, Mr. Skene at his left, he told them of his suspicions.

These Frenchmen were plainly not Acadians, nor traders, nor trappers. By their own story they had come from Quebec, but they had no passports from the governor of Canada. The only papers found on them were certificates from Bishop Saint Vallier of Quebec, to the effect that they had duly received the sacrament. As far as could be made out, they pretended to have escaped from Quebec, but they really b'elonged to Old France, and they had killed two Indians on their way to this place. It was a strange tale with which his Honour acquainted the Council.

'It is my belief,' he ended, 'that they are spies sent out to discover the state of the town and garrison, or else to entice our troops to desert. What is your advice in regard to them, gentlemen?'

'With submission, your Honour,' replied Mr. Adams, 'in my view, they should be immediately put in ward and examined separately as to the truth of their allegations.'

'They are already in custody,' replied the governor. 'Is it your pleasure that they should be interrogated?'

A murmur of assent ran round the board.
The governor rang a small hand-bell. Sergeant Danielson appeared in the doorway.

'Bring in the prisoner who seems the
oldest, the tall man with the black hair.'

It was only a step from the governor's
house to the guardroom. The door had
hardly closed before it opened again to admit the sergeant and file with their prisoner. He was a tall, thin man with a military
carriage; his head nearly touched the low
ceiling; his face, tanned by sun and wind,
was lined with want of sleep and purple
with cold; a four days' beard covered his
cheeks; his long hair, undressed and not
even tied, fell to his shoulder. His air was
haggard, as of a man pursued. His dress
was a medley of the European and the
savage. Over what remained of a long-
skirted coat of fine cloth he wore a fringed
buckskin hunting-shirt. His velvet breeches were in tatters. His legs were bare,
but he had moccasins on his feet. Wrapped
about him was a red-bordered Indian blan-
ket as protection from the cold; and he
edged as near as possible to the crackling
birch logs in the great open fireplace. The
two soldiers in full uniform who stood at

either side with fixed bayonets in their fire-
locks looked sleek and neat by comparison,
although neither rations nor clothing were
ever plentiful at Fort Anne.

The governor frowned.

'Who and what are you?' he demanded,
'and what is the reason of your coming to
this place?' As the governor said this, he
stared hard at the man.

Mr. Adams translated the question into
French. Mr. Shirreff, at the foot of the
table with standish, sand-box, quills, and
various documents spread out before him,
entered the governor's words in the very
vellum-bound minute book to be seen still
in the Province House at Halifax. This
was the procedure throughout the exam-
ination.

There was a pause. Before answering,
the prisoner considered with himself. Then,
throwing back his head, he spoke with
great deliberation.

'My name is Paul François Dupont de
Veillein, as it appears in the paper before
M. le Sécrétaire. I come of a family of
good report in France'—he smiled faintly
and spread out his hands in a graceful ges-
ture—'well known in the ancient city of

Blois. I was educated at Saint Omer, for my parents designed me for the Church, but when I arrived at the age of seventeen, I exchanged the soutane for the King's uniform, and entered the Regiment Salis-Samade as gentleman cadet. In a few months, my family became reconciled to the change and procured me a commission. I served for three years in Flanders, on the eastern frontier, and in Italy, not, I may say, without distinction. During the month of Septemb'er, 1722, I was on furlough in Paris, devoting myself to the pleasures of the capital.'

He smiled again, and then sighed.

'On the first day of October towards dusk, as I was sitting in a café near the Palais Royal, I received a billet from, as I thought, a lady of my acquaintance, making an immediate appointment at our usual rendezvous. When I reached her door, I noticed a hackney coach before it, waiting in the street. As I turned to knock, I felt my arms clutched from behind by two pairs of hands, and, in spite of my resistance, I was dragged into the coach by two men who appeared to be lackeys of some great house. I still strove to tear myself loose while the carriage was rattling over the cobblestones, as fast as the horses could go, but I could not draw my sword. That night I dined in the Bastille.'

'The Bastille!' echoed the governor, and his face grew harsh. 'You are a criminal then. What was your offence?'

Veillein's black brows gathered.

'I do not know. I was never told. Your Excellency understands what is a *lettre de cachet?* You become obnoxious to some great person who has the ear of the King's minister, or the King's mistress. Perhaps some lady finds your society more agreeable than that of a more powerful admirer. Perhaps you have made an epigram or have scribbled some verses about a person of influence which are taken amiss. Perhaps, in your cups, you have mentioned names too freely. Pouf! a little piece of parchment with the sign-manual, and La Bastille closes her jaws upon you. Men grow gray there, men die, and never a hint of accusation or accuser. But I am resolved'—he raised his voice—'to know the reason of my arrest. I will sue for justice at the foot of the throne.'

'How long were you confined in the Bastille?'

'From October, 1722, to August, 1724, two years all but two months. Two years out of my life! When I was twenty! Picture to yourself, M. le Gouverneur! Two years of an innocent man's life spent in prison! True, the imprisonment was not equally rigorous for all. Some of us were allowed to exercise ourselves in the square. It was there, at tennis, I met my friend, M. Alexandre Poupart de Babour, whom I found again at Quebec and who has accompanied me on this adventure.'

'How were you released?'

'One night I was awakened from my sleep by M. Bellamis, *commissaire ordonnateur,* who showed me an order for my instant removal. As soon as I could dress, I was again placed in a coach, with two soldiers for guard, and driven to the western gate of Paris. There I was met by four mounted men with a led horse. Under this escort I travelled day and night until we reached Havre. I was at once taken on board the *Notre Dame de Rouen,* supply ship, in the stream, and ready to sail for New France. Although we had to wait

three days for a favourable wind, I was so
closely watched that I had no opportunity
of communicating with the shore, or of
making my escape. After a voyage of five
weeks, we reached the River of Canada—
a truly magnificent river—and in four days
more we anchored at Quebec. That is
one of the strongest places in the world.
In all my experience as a soldier, I never
saw a town of such natural strength. Posted
on a cliff, up which a goat could hardly find
its way, with an impassable river on the
left flank, it has a complete *enceinte* and
a cavalier mounted on the highest point—
Quebec can never be taken. But pardon
me!' he bowed to the governor and the
Council, 'I forget I am talking to English
officers.'

'How long did you remain in Quebec,
M. de Veillein?'

'About a twelvemonth! I was entertained like a gentleman for that time by the
governor himself, M. de Vaudreuil. Why,
I do not know. That also is to be explained, but I suppose it was upon private
advice from some one who had known me
in Old France. I have no certainty.'

At this point the governor, Mr. Adams,

and Mr. Skene put their heads together and whispered. The prisoner warmed his hands at the fire.

'This is very strange, M. de Veillein, or whatever your name is,' said the governor in a grating voice. 'You were well entertained, you say, by the governor himself, and yet you left the place without his passport. You stole away like a vagabond, like a thief in the night.'

The prisoner bit his lip.

'M. de Vaudreuil is a very old man, near eighty, I should say, and hard to deal with. I tried more than once to obtain a passport, but he always refused it. At the same time he would say: "You may go if you choose, M. de Veillein, whenever you please. I will not stop you;" and his wrinkles would pucker into a smile. I then had recourse to the bishop, M. de Saint Vallier. He could not give me a passport, but you have seen his assurance that I and my two friends were good Catholics and have been regular in our duties.'

Again the three men at the board head consulted in whispers.

'This is also very strange,' said the governor. 'Why did you not sail to Old

France or to the government of Cape Breton?'

'It was not for want of effort,' said the Frenchman. 'I approached the master of every vessel in the port of Quebec. I offered them gold and one or two jewels of some value which I still retained. It was in vain. Not one would receive me on board. You perceive, M. le Gouverneur, the plot of which I am the victim. I was to be banished to the wilderness for ever. It must have been some Great One who could command the governor of Canada, for the governor plainly had his orders, and he controlled every shipmaster in the colony. That Great One having taken a dislike to me was resolved that I should never see France again.'

'But why,' said the governor, still suspicious, 'did you presume to come to this or any English settlement without a passport?'

A faint tinge of answering blood rose in the prisoner's thin cheeks, but his voice was unshaken.

'As I have said, M. le Gouverneur, I come of a family in good repute in France. My father is of the *noblesse,* a chevalier of

Blois. It is not for a man of my blood to submit tamely to such wrongs—to be imprisoned like a malefactor, to be banished from my country; and I was resolved to run all risks in order to reach France again and sue for justice. When I found that it was impossible to leave Quebec with the governor's permission, I cast about for means to escape without it. One day, at the Château Saint Louis, a baptized savage came to pay his respects to the governor. He had been educated in a mission and spoke French well. Some priest, remembering his Virgil, had christened him Aeneas. "Multum ille et terris jactatus et alto," as we say at Saint Omer. He was an old, experienced warrior, who had often been on raids against the English. After the audience was ended, I sought him out. He was in a camp outside the lower town, by the riverside. I sounded him cautiously to find whether he would aid me to escape. He told me of a long way to other French plantations, a long way up and down various rivers, and through forests inhabited only by wild beasts and wild men. I then sought out the other two gentlemen, who have been arrested with me—M. Poupart

de Babour and M. Saint Joli de Pardeithan
—and they agreed eagerly to escape if possible. Among us we made up the sum
Aeneas demanded for acting as guide.
There was some delay after the bargain
was completed, for Aeneas had to make a
canoe large enough to carry five persons.
He had to take his nephew, a young brave,
along to aid him; he could not manage the
canoe by himself.

'On the night of the 28th of August,
there being no moon, we met Aeneas when
the tide served at his camp outside the
lower town. I had got pistols and a musket; M. de Pardeithan had his hanger only,
while M. de Babour brought a fowling-
piece. We took with us also three blan-
kets, some pork and biscuits, and a small
case-bottle of brandy. Our powder-horns
and shot-pouches were filled before starting, and we carried a small reserve of powder in a water-tight canister. Before
embarking. Aeneas insisted on payment
of the thirty pistoles agreed upon, and I
told them into his hand. He bit each piece
and then put it into a belt round his middle.
The ebb aiding us, we paddled down the
river about ten leagues to the mouth of a

river on the south bank, called the *riviere du Sud,* which we reached before daylight. We lay in the woods all that day, rested, ate, and slept. The following night we travelled up this stream for perhaps ten leagues more. Here we carried the canoe and our belongings three leagues through the woods over a well-worn Indian trail, and launched on a river called by Aeneas, Woolstock, but a priest we met in a village called it *rivière Saint Jean.*

'At first all went well. The weather was divine. There were no midges or noxious insects. Our progress was ever downstream. There were few rapids and, consequently, few portages. Aeneas and his nephew caught eels and sea trout and shot partridges and ducks for the *pot-à-feu.* They knew where to halt for the night at the good camping places, near springs of water. Monsieur has seen the *rivière Saint Jean?*'

The governor shook his head.

'In my campaigns,' the prisoner continued. 'I have seen the rivers of France and I have seen the Rhine, but I have never beheld the equal of this stream. I have talked with M. de Pardeithan, who has traversed the Mississippi, the Ohio, and the River of Canada, also in canoe. He had never seen anything so beautiful, though in the River of Canada there is a great lake with many islands—a thousand, he said—which is enchanting. Figure to yourself, monsieur, long smooth reaches broadening into placid lakes, now flat terraces near the mouths of the tributary streams, some twenty-five toises in height. The river banks and the distant hills on either hand were like fires of yellow and crimson, for, as you know, autumn in this country turns the leaves to marvelous hues. And the skies—of such height! such blueness! Only the nights were cold and grew ever colder.

'The Indians talked much of a great village and fort on this river, called Meductec, which we were continually approaching. We had reached a camping ground about fifty leagues above this settlement on the 10th of September. For some days, we had noticed a change in the demeanour of the two Indians; they were growing careless and insolent, slow to answer if one of us spoke to them, and always consulting together in their own tongue. From some words M. de Pardeithan overheard, it ap-

33

peared that they had formed the design of stealing away in the canoe and abandoning us in the wilderness, where, without such guides, we must have perished with hunger. They were weary of convoying us and acting as our servants; and they had received their payment. That afternoon, when we halted to camp and the Indians were fishing, we became convinced of their treachery, and we resolved to seize the canoe at dawn.

'That night we slept little. Each of us watched in turn while pretending to sleep, and waked the others so quietly that the Indians did not observe our stratagem. Just as the first light broke in the east, I roused my two comrades cautiously. We had scarcely risen to our feet when the Indians sprang up also, perceiving our design. There was a scuffle. The young brave, being the most nimble, leaped on M. de Pardeithan and bore him to the ground. Aeneas dropped on one knee and levelled his piece. I fired my pistol at him as he pulled the trigger. I felt his bullet whistle past my ear, but he fell face downward. M. de Babour, seeing the other Indian about to stab our friend, clapped the fowling-piece to his ear and shot him dead.

'It was all over in a few moments of time. Aeneas lay groaning on the ground, but beyond seeing or feeling. The young brave's head was a blackened mass of blood and brains and smouldering hair. M. de Pardeithan rose to his feet slowly, and we three stood there, speechless, breathing heavily, in the dim morning light beside the dead camp-fire, with the bodies of our enemies at our feet.

'That, M. le Gouverneur, is the truth concerning this slaying, on the faith of a Christian.'

'What did you do then?'

'In a few minutes the groans of Aeneas ceased, but we remained where we stood, without moving, in the midst of a great silence. Then some one laughed loud and long, like an overwrought woman, who will presently weep and shriek. It was M. de Babour, who is a mere boy. He was staring like a madman at the young brave's head—one eye had been blown out of its socket, and lay by itself on the grass—and he was laughing, laughing. It was an hour before we could quiet him.

'As soon as we recovered our wits, we put all the gear of the dead Indians in the canoe and stripped them mother naked. This shirt belonged to Aeneas; this hole was made by my bullet. Then we carried the bodies into the forest about two hundred yards, and scraped a shallow trench with our knives and our hands. I made a little cross of twigs to lay on the breast of each, for, though savages, they were christened men. Then we covered them over with earth and concealed the grave with leaves and brushwood as well as we could. It would not, we knew, mislead any Indian who might follow in our track, but we could not leave the corpses where they fell. The sun was at noon before we had finished our task and had left, I hope for ever, that accursed spot.

'Picture to yourself, M. le Gouverneur, our plight: without a guide in the heart of the wild, not daring to retrace our steps to Quebec, knowing nothing of what lay before us, our food and ammunition low. Besides, we feared the vengeance of the tribe, for the two men that we had slain. M. de Pardeithan had told us how Indians treated captives. He had witnessed scenes the account of which made our blood run cold.'

'But did you meet with no Indians on your journey down the river?' asked the governor.

'No. God is good. Not till we reached St. John.'

'Did you not see Indians at Meductec?'

'No, your Excellency, and for this reason: Aeneas had spoken so often of this great village of his people that we were very wary. Late one afternoon we saw smoke in the sky far downstream. So we landed, laid the canoe up in the bushes, and waited till night. When it was quite dark we set out again, keeping very close to the eastern bank, and so passed undetected in the darkness.'

'But you met with Indians at St. John, you say. Did they not recognize the canoe and question you about the owner?'

'Your Excellency will remember that it was a new canoe, made for the journey, and only finished just before we left Quebec. None but ourselves had seen it.'

'When did you reach St. John?'

'About three weeks ago. We are unskilful with the paddle and unversed in the

craft of the hunter and the woodman. Our
progress was slow. We went in continual
dread of the Indians. M. de Pardeithan,
having great experience in America, was
our mainstay. He shot the game and caught
the fish and cooked the meals. At last we
reached St. John.

'Here we found Père Gaulin of the Mis-
sions Etrangères. To him we made our
confession and received absolution. At the
first opportunity we heard mass. He as-
sisted us in every way and instructed us
how to reach the French settlements farther on, for we dared not remain at St.
John. A party of Indians was going to
Beaubassin; he recommended us to their
care. So they piloted us to the river of
Beaubassin, where there is a prodigious
tide. Here we dared not stay, for fear the
tribe of Aeneas would discover his death
and hunt us down. We learned that there
was another French settlement, called
Mines, about twenty-five leagues farther
on, which could be reached by water. After
a rest of two days, we set out again along
the coast. We were much buffeted by the
strong tides and currents which run like a
mill-race. We reached a great meadow

overlooked by a mighty cape. Here were many houses amid orchards and cultivated fields, from which the harvest had been gathered. The watercourses were diked against the sea. So fair a prospect I had not looked on since I quitted France.

'Here at last, I thought, we had found a safe haven, but our hopes were dashed. No sooner had we disclosed the dreadful story to the elders of the village, than they manifested the greatest terror and ordered us to depart immediately. They would not suffer us to remain there another night. They assured us that the Indians would track us down and destroy us with all the torments of hell. To afford us food or shelter might bring the savages to cut their throats. The only place of safety was with you, M. le Gouverneur, under your protection, here in your strong fort. So the elders assured us, but they would not harbour us another hour if they could help it. Nor would any villager dare to act as our guide. So once more, we set forth along an unknown coast in this cold and snow. All our previous sufferings were nothing to what we have endured these last five days. We could make no headway against the adverse tides, but were forced to land and await the ebb. We slept on the bare ground under the canoe. Our last morsel of bread we shared yesterday at noon. We are men in the last extremity. Another twenty-four hours and we must have died of cold and hunger.

'We throw ourselves upon your Excellency's mercy. If you turn us away, we must perish miserably from cold and hunger, or fall victims to the cruelty of the savages.'

There was a pause. The governor asked to see the minutes the secretary had taken down; and the big book was passed up to him. While he consulted the entries, there was silence in the room, except for the crackling of the fire. The prisoner never took his eyes off the governor's face. The book was handed back to the secretary.

'Answer me one more question,' said the governor. 'Are not you and your two friends deserters from the troops at Quebec?'

'On the faith of a Christian, your Excellency'—the prisoner laid his hand on his heart—'we are not. I scorn to deny that I myself hold the King's commission in the

Regiment Salis-Samade. I have already informed your Excellency that I have served in Old France. But my friends were never in the army. I have greater acquaintance with M. de Babour than with M. de Pardeithan, for we were both prisoners in the Bastille together, and little better than prisoners again at Queb'ec. M. de Pardeithan I have known only some four months, since he came to Canada from the Mississippi. I—we—the heat—'

The tall Frenchman swayed where he stood, and would have fallen forward with his face against the table, if Sergeant Danielson and one of the soldiers had not caught him in time and laid him on the floor. He was in a dead faint. The Council started from their seats. Mr. Skene ran to the Frenchman's side and put a hand over his heart.

'Brandy!' he cried. 'At once!'

Mr. Doucett opened a locker and produced a glass and a square bottle. The surgeon forced some of the liquor through the clenched teeth of the prostrate man.

'Far gone,' Mr. Skene muttered, as he felt in his pocket for his lancet; 'ill nourished—vital forces weak.' He opened a vein in the Frenchman's arm and administered more brandy. Presently the prisoner revived sufficiently to open his eyes, but he could not sit up, though he tried hard to do so. The soldiers propped him on his feet and half carried him back to the guardroom. At Mr. Skene's suggestion, the governor ordered food for him.

The investigation was not abandoned on account of this occurrence. The guard next brought M. de Pardeithan before the Council. He proved to be a thick-set, sad-eyed Breton. His thin, delicate hands were calloused and chilblained, but on one grimy finger was a seal ring with his arms engraved upon it. This he showed to the governor in proof of his gentle blood. His evidence confirmed the story of M. de Veillein in every particular. Of himself, he said that he had been transported to New Spain, for his share in a fatal duel in which he had seconded a friend. From New Spain, he had escaped to the French plantations at the mouth of the Mississippi, where he had obtained employment as secretary. After remaining in this post for three years, he had made his way up the great river to its affluent, the Ohio, and so by the lakes and the River of Canada to Quebec. He had traversed the continent from south to north. All he knew of the other prisoners was the account they gave of themselves, and that they were respected in Quebec as gentlemen.

The third prisoner, M. Alexandre Poupart de Babour, a famished blond Cupidon of twenty, in dirty rags, agreed in every respect with the other two. He did not know the real cause of his confinement in the Bastille, nor of his transportation to Canada, but he believed that it had been so ordered by some of his family, on account of amours, for he had been a very wild youth.

The prayer of the three adventurers was not refused. They were detained within the walls of Fort Anne for six months as prisoners on parole. The officers supplied them with clothing and welcomed them to their table. During the dull winter days and long winter evenings, the strangers learned to speak English. In a hundred agreeable ways, they helped to pass the time, at cards or chess, or with stories, over the wine, of Old France—campaigns, travels, duels, love affairs—of the wild countries of New Spain and Louisiana. The place had known no such winter since the Sieur de Champlain instituted the Order of Good Cheer in 1606, as related in the pages of Master Marc Lescarbot.

In the spring, Mr. William Winniett, trading up the bay, made inquiries at Mines, learned that the Frenchmen's tale was true, and wrote to the Hon. John Doucett to tell him so. He and the Council then agreed that their guests were not spies, but gentlemen who had met with misfortunes and ill usage. They further agreed that to detain them at Annapolis Royal until the Indians began to gather there would be mere cruelty. So by the very earliest opportunity, they were shipped off to Boston, and the annals of Nova Scotia know them no more.

What happened after their arrival in Boston—whether they ever saw France again and obtained that justice from Louis le Bien-aimé which de Veillein was determined to sue for—remains a mystery.

II

The Payzant Captivity

II

The Payzant Captivity

N the present year of grace 1912 there may be seen any day in the streets of Halifax a man of threescore and ten whom you would remember without difficulty the next time you met him. In spite of his seventy years and his thick, white, close-cropped hair and moustache, it would be a misuse of words to call him old. Over six feet tall, erect, spare, athletic, with an open-air complexion, he might easily be taken for a half-pay officer still hale and vigorous. By profession he is a lawyer still in active practice, and his name is prominent in directorates of banks and joint-stock companies. His ample means permit the pleasure of foreign travel, but he prefers to a winter in Rome a long summer in his camp beside a salmon river. His favourite reading is theology and church history. Altogether, John Y. Payzant is the sort of man you would turn round in the street to look at on his own account. If you knew how he links the present with the heroic age of Canada, you would not be content with a single glance.

His grandfather, Louis Payzant, as a boy of ten, was a prisoner in Quebec in 1759, and witnessed from the ramparts the world-famous battle on the Plains of Abraham, which decided the fate of America. Three generations span the intervening century and a half. The Payzants are a long-lived race.

The story begins in Normandy, in the ancient city of Caen, at the time of the revocation of the Edict of Nantes. Payzant, as you might imagine, is a French name, and the earliest traceable bearer of it, belonging to the obnoxious faction of the Huguenots, was forced, with thousands of other good Frenchmen, to abjure his faith or flee the country. He took refuge in the Island of Jersey and there apparently prospered. In the year 1754 his son Louis, who owned three ships, sold two and betook himself in the third, with his young wife, little sons and all his worldly goods, to the new 'boom' town of Halifax, in Nova Scotia, just planted amid the spruce forest on the shore of Chebucto Harbour. He brought with him letters of introduction from Pownall to Governor Lawrence, the man who expelled the Acadians. Lawrence, in turn, passed him on to Colonel Sutherland, who was in charge of the German settlement of Lunenburg, farther down the coast, near the beautiful Mahone Bay, which is currently believed to have an island in it for every day in the year.

One of these islands, now called Covey's, the newcomer selected for his home and set to work with energy to make it habitable. Two years went swiftly by. The first rude shelter for the wood-cutters, a sort of brush wigwam, had given place to a solid log cabin. Bales and boxes of goods for trading with the Indians had been brought and stored within it. But this was not sufficient for the needs of the trader and the head of a family. A large two-storey frame house had soon been begun, a clearing had been made and sown with fall wheat, and all went well until the spring of 1756. The year before, Braddock had been routed with great slaughter on the banks of the Monongahela, and the Acadians had been deported from Nova Scotia. Halifax was put in a posture of defence and her first privateers had sailed out past Thrum Cap in quest of lawful prizes. The Seven Years' War had begun and was to drag into its fatal net this prosperous beginning of a pioneer's home near the border of the western wilderness.

It was the eighth of May, 1756. All over the clearing among the raw stumps the wheat was springing green. The men at work on the new house had gone to their homes in Lunenburg, three miles away. Peaceful night had fallen, and the Payzant family were getting ready for b'ed, when they heard a strange noise not far away. What could it mean? The father thought he knew what it betokened. There had been serious disaffection in the new German settlement of Lunenburg, on the hog's-back headland overlooking Malagash harbor just round the corner from Mahone. Unprepared for the rigours of life in the wilderness, these peasants from the Palatinate had thought themselves wronged and had risen in some sort of half-hearted, futile rebellion. Payzant, as a friend of the Government, had been warned to be on his guard, and had been given licence to fire upon any disturbers of the peace. Little dreaming that he had to do with an Indian war party, he stepped to the door with his musket and fired in the air to frighten the intruders. The flash from the muzzle in the darkness revealed his position to the enemy; in answer, a shattering volley rang out on the night and stretched him, a dying man, across his own threshold. His wife rushed out to catch him as he fell. He could only gasp out a few half-choked words in French, 'My heart is growing cold—the Indians—,' before the spirit passed and the rush of the whooping savages drove his wife back into the house. Somehow she managed to bolt and bar the door, which was stout enough to resist all efforts to break it in.

Without warning, in a moment of time, irreparable calamity had befallen the settler's home; the father was dead, and the helpless widow and her children were huddled together in an inner room, unable to realize the tragedy, quaking with fear, and not knowing what minute the murderers would burst in upon them, tomahawk and scalping-knife in hand.

While they awaited their doom, the Indians, baffled at the main entrance, managed to get into the room occupied by a serving-woman and her child. Her they did to death in some horrible unknown fashion, tore off her scalp, and dashed out the baby's brains. On the other side of the partition, Marie Payzant and her children heard the terrifying uproar of the struggle, the yells of the Indians, the agonized shrieks of the poor creature with death before her eyes, her vain appeals for help to her master and mistress: 'Mr. Payzant! Mrs. Payzant!'

When these cries ceased, the Indians renewed their efforts to break into the last poor refuge, but apparently the stout, well-mortised logs of the cabin still defied them. At last they made ready to burn it down, and then the despairing woman gave the word to her eldest son, Philip, to unbar the door. He drew the bolt and the Indians rushed in.

At that moment the mother at least must have felt the bitterness of death, but, strange to say, the Indians spared her and her children. One would think that scalps would be as profitable as prisoners, and much easier to transport, and, further, that the savage blood-thirst would not be so soon quenched. Their hands were still red with the blood of one woman and her child; but these others they did not attempt to harm. Philip, the eldest boy, sprang on a table, shook his fist at them and defied them, and yet they did not touch him. Who can understand the workings of the savage mind? One horrid detail of this time has been transmitted. As a sort of diabolical joke, the Indians mimicked the cries of the poor serving-woman and her vain appeals to 'Mr. Payzant! Mrs. Payzant!' Not blood but plunder seems to have been their object, after they got into the house, and they set to work to sack the trader's stores.

That scene of pillage and confusion was never forgotten by the boy of seven years. When he was ninety-five, his body bent and his mental faculties lulled into passivity by his great age, he was roused to intense excitement by his memories of that tragic night. Raising himself to his full height, he cried to his questioner:

'Oh, I see them! I hear them! Hewing down the boxes, hewing down the boxes.'

The trader's store would offer the kind

of spoil most desired by the savages. They hastily ransacked the house and took their plunder to the canoes, along with their prisoners, the new-made widow and the four fatherless children.

One more victim remained to be sacrificed. Earlier in the day the war party had surprised two settlers, father and son, on Rous' Island, at the other side of Mahone Bay. They killed the father and forced the boy to guide them among the maze of islands to Payzant's home. Although they had promised to spare the boy's life and let him go unharmed, they murdered him by the waterside in the sight of Marie Payzant and her children, and took his scalp. Colonel Sutherland and his rangers were in Lunenburg, only three miles away, and he might have given the alarm. When the soldiers came next morning they found the poor boy's dead body with the hands still bound. What he must have endured that last day of his life from the hour of his father's death till he saw the lifted tomahawks is beyond all telling. After the last murder, the Indians fired the plundered cabin and pushed off in the darkness. The last sight the captives had of their home was a mass of leaping flames against the gloom. Their feelings anyone with a heart can call up. Of Marie Payzant, widowed in an instant, stunned by the scenes she had just witnessed, carried off to an unknown fate, with the mother's time of trial impending, it is recorded that 'tears would not come to her relief.'

Mahone Bay is about four hundred miles from the city of Queb'ec, as you measure with a ruler and dividers across the map. The weary road the captives travelled to reach Quebec was well-nigh twice as long.

During the night of the 8th-9th of May the war party, with their prisoners, or 'ransomers,' as they were then called, paddled across the bay to where the pretty summer town of Chester now stands. From this point to the head waters of the St. Croix is a twelve-mile stretch through the woods. The little stream known as Gold River may have shortened the portage to the Ponhook Lakes. Still, how they managed to transport their canoes, their plunder, and their captives so quickly through the forest remains something of a mystery. Evidently the road was known to them, if they were not actually returning by the way they had

come, and they no longer needed a guide.
It is also plain from their haste that they
feared pursuit. On the following night,
twenty-four hours after the descent upon
the Payzant household, the canoes were
gliding past Fort Edward, where the St.
Croix empties into the Avon, fifty miles
away. This was a British fort, on the high
hill above Windsor, keeping watch over the
wasted Acadian parishes from which Murray had swept the habitants the year before. As they floated by in silence, the
captives could see against the sky the sil-
houette of the unsuspecting sentry pacing
the ramparts. Friends and safety were
near, but the captives dared not give the
alarm. A tomahawk, flourished over their
heads, warned them silently what their
fate would be upon the faintest outcry. The
canoes drew in close to the bank and so
passed unseen and unchallenged in the
darkness. When the day broke they were
out of sight on their way to Cape Chignecto, fifty miles further on. Only when they
reached this point did they make their first
halt. They had covered a hundred miles
without sleep or rest, and probably with
little food. It was this extraordinary

swiftness of movement that made an Indian raid so incalculable and so feared.

No record has been preserved of the time occupied by the long journey to Quebec. If the Indians succeeded in covering the fifty miles between the island of massacre and Fort Edward in the short period of twenty-four hours, they might, at this rate, have reached their ultimate destination in a fortnight. But they would not proceed at such a rate; this first stage was a forced march through an enemy's country, where they were always in danger. When they reached French territory they would travel more slowly. They must have halted for some time at St. Ann's, the present Fredericton, and the whole good summer season was before them.

Their route is worth considering, for they followed an ancient and well-used system of inland waterways which connected the St. Lawrence and the interior of the continent with the sea. From Chignecto, they would paddle up to Petitcodiac, past the site of busy Moncton; then they would portage from its head-waters to the source of the Kennebecasis, and, favoured by current, would soon reach its junction with the beautiful River St. John. This magnificent stream is four hundred miles from mouth to source. From its head there was an inconsiderable portage to the Chaudière, which empties into the St. Lawrence from the south bank, almost opposite the city of Quebec.

One pathetic little incident of the journey has been handed down. Among the plunder, Marie Payzant recognized the very shoes she had worn as a happy bride in far-off peaceful Jersey. She may have danced in them at her wedding. She had brought them with her across the Atlantic and treasured them with a woman's love of keepsakes all these years. By some strange chance they had escaped the burning house; and now the widow saw them again, with what feelings may be imagined. She begged her captors for them. The Indians considered them not worth taking farther, and flung them overboard, 'with a loud, insulting laugh.'

At the French post of St. Ann's a new trial awaited her. Up to this time, though husbandless and a prisoner, Marie Payzant had her children with her; now she was separated from them and sent on by herself to Queb'ec. Some time after reaching the city her child was born, a second daughter, who was named Lizette; but months went by without word of what had befallen the others. At last news came that two were in the hands of the French, but that two were still detained by the Indians, for adoption into the tribe. The two white children were to fill the places of children who had been killed by the English. One was the mother's namesake, Marie. Their release was effected with no little difficulty. It was only when Bishop Pontbriand, in response to the mother's entreaties, directed the priest at St. Ann's to refuse the Indians absolution that the obstinate savages surrendered the children.

For some months they must have run wild about the post or in the forest, and certain childish recollections of that stay in St. Ann's have been transmitted. When asked what they were fed on, old Louis Payzant exclaimed:

'Fed us upon! Why, sometimes bread, and sometimes nothing.'

One night his piece of bread was so bad as to be uneatable and he threw it away. No more was given him; that night he must go hungry. But the Indian's son, of his own age, was given for supper a larger piece than he could eat. As he fell asleep, the bread slipped from his hand, and young Payzant devoured it. In the morning, the little Indian missed his breakfast and complained to his father, who was just setting out to fish. The old Indian was furious, and threatened young Payzant with some dire punishment, but he never lived to carry out his threat. That day he got drunk, fell out of his canoe, and was drowned. Louis Payzant also remembered being carried through the woods by this Indian, alternately with his own son. 'He would take me by the shoulders and swing me round upon his back, while the other youngster trotted behind.' He had also memories, which plainly could not have belonged to the spring season, of going in the canoe to gather berries. From all that can be learned, it seems that the Indians treated the white children like their own, no better and no worse.

Altogether, the separation of Marie Payzant from her children lasted seven months. At the end of that time they, with other luckless British prisoners, were brought in to Quebec. When Marie heard of their arrival she was eager with all a mother's impatience to go to them at once. But this was not permitted. There were other captive women as well as she, awaiting the coming of their children. She was forced to wait at the door of her lodgings, under military guard, while the troop of little 'ransomers' was brought up from which to choose her own. It was no hard task, though doubtless they were an unkempt b'and, in sore need of a mother's care. The tears that would not come to her relief, when the first stunning blow fell, now flowed free as she strained her darlings to her breast.

So there the family remained more than four years, until after the fall of Quebec. They lived through the times of sickness, cold, and privation, and the terrors of the English bombardment which laid the city in ruins. Apparently the women and children were not, like the men, kept in close confinement in the French soldiers' barracks. There was no danger that they would escape. The children picked up the language and perhaps some education. When a grandfather, Louis Payzant would take his grandson on his knee and teach him the Lord's Prayer in French. No doubt the boys had the run of the town, and with many of the citizens saw from the walls the two-hours' fight of September 13 and the retreat of the white-coat battalions on the gate of St. Louis. A family tradition tells that a French soldier tried to prevent young Louis from getting a place on the wall, but the boy evaded him. Six days after the battle, the prison doors in Quebec opened for all the captives, and the worst of the Payzants' troubles were over.

By August, 1761, Marie Payzant was back in Halifax with her five children, receiving official permission to dispose of the tragic island in Mahone Bay, and obtaining grants of land about Falmouth, where her descendants dwell to this day.

As soon as the news of the Payzant killing had been brought into Lunenburg, Sutherland had dispatched an officer and thirty men to make sure of the facts and, if possible, punish the raiders. They found only pitiable corpses with the scalps torn off and the smoking ruins of the settler's home. The blow had been struck without warning and the assailants had vanished without leaving behind them the slightest trace as to whence they had come or whither they had gone. Sutherland reported to Lawrence, and the insolent daring of the Indians enraged the governor, at no time the mildest of men. Six days after the massacre he issued a proclamation, protesting indignantly against the way the Micmacs had broken their treaty of four years previous, 'expressly against the law of arms,' as Fluellen would say. He therefore authorised and commanded all King George's liege subjects to 'annoy, distress, take and destroy the Indians' inhabiting the different parts of the Province; and, in order to make war support war, he offered the substantial sum of thirty pounds for every Indian prisoner about the age of sixteen brought in alive, twenty-five for his scalp, and the same amount for every Indian woman or child brought in alive. These bounties seem excessive, but probably they represent the current rates for such commodities on both the French and the English side. Lawrence was probably mistaken in thinking that the Indians were Micmacs belonging to the province.

The fact that they needed a guide to the house of a settler who had been in the province for two years, and that the two Payzant children were detained near St. Ann's, would indicate that the war-band were Malicetes raiding across from French territory, and that they had their hunting-grounds about the upper reaches of the St. John.

Apparently not many pounds were paid in this gruesome way suggested by Lawrence. Years afterwards, Louis Payzant recognized in his store in Halifax a member of the very war-party which had descended on his home in blood and fire.

'You are one of the Indians who killed my father,' he said.

'Well,' was the reply, 'I am, but it was war then.'

This is what an Indian raid meant. The early pages of Canadian history are fairly free from such blood-stains, but for many years the western frontier of the American colonies presented countless scenes of similar murder and rapine.

As near as can be sifted out from written record and oral tradition, this is the truth about the Payzant killing. Good old Silas

THE PAYZANT CAPTIVITY

Rand, the apostle of the Micmacs, took down the tale from the lips of Louis Payzant himself in his ninety-fifth year, and on this account the present narrative is mainly based. Time has raised a goodly growth of myth around the original facts. It is commonly believed that Marie Payzant was well treated during her captivity at Quebec because she was the sister of Montcalm; and in Lunenburg is still to be seen a stone, marked with an outspread bloody hand, the sign-manual of one of the murderers.

III

A 'Ransomer' of Montcalm's

at Levis began to rain solid shot and bursting shell upon the devoted city, all these

III

A 'Ransomer' of Montcalm's

HEN the frigates and transports
of Admiral Saunders were
moored before Quebec and
General James Wolfe was
ranging up and down Montcalm's impreg-
nable lines, searching for some weak spot
to break through, these operations caused
acute discomfort to nine English prisoners
in the besieged city. The nine unfortunates
were crowded together in one room of the
barracks, fourteen feet long by eight broad,
which contained, besides their 'small necessities,' three beds. The space remaining
for air, movement, and comfort may be
easily computed. Their rations—prisoner's fare—, which were poor and scanty at
the best of times, were reduced when the
city was invested; for all Quebec, soldiers,
as well as citizens, suffered from famine.
Cold, close confinement, slow starvation,
sickness were the lot of the captives, but
when the British batteries across the river

at Levis began to rain solid shot and bursting shell upon the devoted city, all these calamities were forgotten in the deadly fear of a sudden, horrible death. Few situations can try human fortitude more severely than that of being penned helplessly in a death-trap and fired on by unwitting friends. Worse than any dreadful certainty is the long-drawn agony of suspense. So, day by day, and hour by hour, these wretched men were forced to abide their fate, as the cannonade thundered from Levis, never knowing when one of the deadly missiles, which were laying Quebec in ruins, should find their miserable cell and shatter them to mere blood-boltered rags of humanity.

These brothers in distress had been gathered together by wide sweeps of the French net. There was Mr. Hawes, an officer of the Province ship from Boston, who had gone to defend Georges against the Indians. He had been captured in a barge with eleven of his men near the Fox Islands in Penobscot Bay. He had spent nearly a year in captivity, and deliverance was now close at hand at Quebec, when he took a great fever, went to hospital and died

there, like many another poor fellow. There
was Captain Mayors from Boston. The
year before, he had been bound up the Bay
of Fundy, with a fine cargo for Annapolis
Royal, when a privateer manned by exiled
Acadians pounced upon him. His vessel
was taken to Petitcodiac, where she was
laid up, while he and his crew were sent on
to Quebec. Next year, the welcome news
reached him in prison that his ship had been
retaken by an English force. In spite of
'a great purging,' which sent him to the
deadly hospital for three weeks, Mayors
survived the siege. Let us hope that he
got his vessel back and recovered com-
pensation for his losses. Captain Graw
from Old York had also been captured in
the Bay. He was the commander of a
large 'scunner,' laden with lime. His mate
and at least two of his crew died in captivity. Captain Sweatland was the master
of a schooner from St. Martin's, laden with
oil and salt, which was captured off the
Banks. He and his men had been brought
in about the end of May, 1759; so his term
of imprisonment lasted barely four months.
There were also two other sea-captains,
Wally and Hob'orn, a Mr. Sandford, or

Stadford, from Bristol and a young lad called Thomas Colley, a 'ransomer,' or prisoner. Of these, the record has handed down no more than the names.

That any details at all have been preserved is due to the ninth man, John Witherspoon, another 'ransomer.' Raiding even on a small scale and snatching even single noncombatants seems to have been part of the French policy to wear down English resistance. Witherspoon belongs to the noble army of diarists to whom the world is so deeply in debt. Hailing like Captain Graw and the double traitor John Clark from Old York in Maine, he had taken up land, probably a deserted Acadian farm, in the beautiful valley of the Annapolis in Nova Scotia. On the fourteenth of September, 1757, as he was cutting wood on the South Mountain near the fort, he had been surprised by a war-party of Indians raiding into Nova Scotia from the French territory beyond the Tantramar. He was not the first victim of Indian stealth and daring. The year before, a war-band of Malicetes had killed six settlers in one day and carried off five prisoners from Mahone, within three miles of a garrisoned settlement; and now Witherspoon was snatched under the very guns of the fort. His Journal makes mention of other prisoners, regular soldiers, rangers, officers no less than privates, as well as peaceful settlers like himself, waylaid, seized, and dragged off to the horrors of captivity. Somehow or other, Witherspoon managed to obtain a 'small pamphlet,' or blank book, in which he kept a rough journal of his life as a prisoner, writing in tobacco-juice, when ink failed. This record has survived the writer and all his adventures. Once when the prison at Quebec was closely searched for all papers and writing materials, everything was taken, except 'this small pamphlet of mine,' which had been hidden under the straw bed, when the jailor's back was turned. Some thirty years ago, a transcript of the original was published by a local historical society, with all its imperfections on its head. The printer made mistakes; no doubt the transcriber made mistakes; some of the original was lost; much of it was defaced and all was hard to decipher. But with all its faults, it is a valuable record, this strangely inscribed bit of flotsam borne down the stream of time.

It offers the authentic portraiture of a
human soul and it reveals the dangers of a
settler's life in the early days and the grim
realities of a prisoner's lot in the hard-
hearted eighteenth century.

In character, Witherspoon was, first and
foremost, a militant Puritan. His piety is
shown by his long meditations on his
troubles, meditations which are mosaics of
Bible texts. If he had not his pocket Bible
with him, he had made good use of it be-
forehand; his memory is stored with long
passages from the Scriptures. He finds
consolation in the Book of Job. A shock
of earthquake startles his conscience. He
was genuinely offended at breaches of the
third commandment by the soldiers, by
'blackguard discourse,' by the idleness and
lying of the French, by the drunkenness of
his fellow-prisoners on one memorable occasion. He was a good husband and father,
lamenting repeatedly his separation from
his dear wife and family, which caused him,
in his own phrase, 'many a melancholy
hour.' He was also a good patriot, pray-
ing like any Ironside for the success of 'our
army,' and imploring the aid of the God of
Battles, 'who has stiled himself a man of

74

war.' He was not an educated man; his grammar and spelling are quite unfettered by convention; but he has the great virtue of being an honest man, who sets down plainly what he sees and hears. Literary embellishment is happily beyond him, but sometimes by dint of his very downrightness he has phrases that stick fast in the memory. His reference to the prisoners, 'looking through these Iron grates like so many malefactors till our cheek Bones are grown thine,' reveals in a flash the long misery of bondage. Once, at least, he is unconsciously humorous, when he notes, 'it pleased God to visit me with a very generous cold and a soer throat.' He must have had strength of mind; keeping a diary is one proof; and his original dietary of milk is another.

Peering through his iron grates in his barrack cell, Witherspoon saw as much of that great drama, the Fall of New France, as was possible for a prisoner to see. He could see the men-of-war passing up and down the broad St. Lawrence, French fire-ships blazing in the night, flotillas of boats, the smoke of distant firing, and he could hear the rattle of the fusilade and the boom

of cannon. He could wonder what it all
meant and try to piece out scraps of information from the jailor, or the doctor,
or, perhaps, a prisoner who had just been
brought in. What he finds out, he sets
down with the directness of Defoe, and his
journal notes just those small particulars of
life in a besieged city which the big serious
histories omit. It is during the siege that
the entries are fullest and most picturesque.

How he got to Quebec is a story by itself. The first entry in the journal tells
of his arrival at Miramichi on the 16th of
November, 1757, having reached Petitcodiac on the 7th of the same month. He
remained at Miramichi until the following
August, when he was sent, with a whole
batch of prisoners, round by water to Quebec. The fall of Louisbourg and the
weakening of the garrison at this post made
their detention difficult. Some had almost
succeeded in making their escape.

'Liberty being a thing that none knows
how to price but those that are deprived
of it,' is Witherspoon's view of this natural
and inalienable right. The lightest captivity is galling, but captivity in the eighteenth century meant life reduced to its low-

est terms. It meant the minimum of food
and shelter that would keep a man's soul
in his body. Of this Witherspoon offers
abundant evidence. He and his friends did
not propose to remain prisoners, if they had
a chance to escape. Under the date June
17, he notes that the time was ripe. The
French garrison was weak, and the com-
mandant had transferred the prisoners to
a new and, presumably, stronger prison,
being 'jealous,' writes Witherspoon, using
the word in its Shakespearian sense of 'suspicious,' 'lest we should take an opportunity and make our escape.' The plans of
the captives were simple, but an amount of
furtive, whispered plotting in the dark of
the new prison, and of discussion, arrange-
ment and rearrangement of details must
have gone to their making. Out of their
scanty rations the prisoners put aside a
part as provision for the journey, and they
had a certain big canoe in their eye that
would hold them all. The canoe once secured, they would work down the coast as
fast as they could to Baie Verte. Once
across the Musquash they would be safe in
British territory and could easily make
their way to Fort Lawrence on the west

side of the isthmus of Chignecto. The whole distance was about two hundred miles, for they would have to hug the shore. With a good start, determined men might have done it in three days. The war-party that carried off Mrs. Payzant and her children from Mahone Bay covered fifty miles, including portages, in twenty-four hours.

On the tenth of July about two o'clock in the morning, the prisoners succeeded in breaking out of their jail, secured the big canoe, and paddled off without being detected. Witherspoon's own words best tell what happened: 'We set out with a good heart. We wrought very hard all that day. We made a very good run of it to the distance of near forty leagues. But night coming on some of our people began to be very cross and surley and would not work. Having some licker on bord som of them drank so freely that they rendered themselves unfit for any service.' By stiff paddling, they had covered about one hundred and twenty miles in eighteen hours or so, and must have been somewhere near Shediac. All through that July day they had maintained a steady six miles per hour; they must have been underfed, cramped in their narrow quarters, aching in every muscle, and irritable for lack of sleep. So the 'licker' proved irresistible. On the second night they could not, or would not paddle, and they failed to make good the advantage they had gained. The exasperated Witherspoon begged them to improve the time, but he had a boat-load of lunatics to deal with. So they drifted, one fancies, through the darkness, with one despairing man to steer, and keep the cockleshell with its freight of drunkards from oversetting.

With the first light of dawn, the watcher saw two white sails coming swiftly down upon them before the strong north wind. The French were on their track and rapidly overhauling them. The portent brought the sots partially at least to their senses. They could not hope to paddle faster than the ships could sail. Escape by water was cut off. Perhaps it was still possible by land. They ran the canoe ashore, hid it in the underbrush, and plunged into the forest, heading ever south and east towards Baie Verte. Some were still so drunk that they could not march, and one craven 'pre-

6

ferred a few things he had brought with him before his liberty,' as Witherspoon notes with proper scorn. The rest must have kept up an anxious watch through the tree trunks; and soon they were dismayed at the sight of the ships coming to anchor quite near them and landing men. More time was wasted discussing what to do and wandering distractedly in the wilderness. At length they came to a decision. They would double back to where the canoe was hidden, 'tarry till the evening,' and try to slip past the French ships in the darkness. It was a likely plan, indeed the only one with the least promise of success. What must have been the rage of the desperate men, when on returning to the place where they had hidden the canoe they found that Johnson Young, the man they had left behind, had delivered up their one means of safety to the French!

It was now about four o'clock in the afternoon, and while they were debating what to do in their extremity, they saw a sight that must have turned them sick and cold in spite of the July weather. Close at hand were four canoes, two filled with French and two with Indians, which had stolen on them unawares. The assailants were all smeared with war-paint, bedecked with feathers, half-naked, white men as well as red, 'looking more like devils than men,' says the journal. Now the fugitives' last hope of escape was gone. The forest could not hide them. The Indians would track them down like bloodhounds on the scent, and then the stake, the fire, the knife awaited them. Death would come only after hours of agony. Still there remained one last chance of saving the bare life. About half a mile away was the hut of a Frenchman, Pierre Surrette. How they came by that bit of information is not stated; perhaps some schooner captain knew the coast. To throw themselves on Surrette's mercy was now their sole chance of salvation. It was just possible that he might be able to protect them against the savages. The little party broke up in distraction, some running this way and some that, through the hot July woods. Witherspoon had not gone far before he almost ran upon the muskets of four Frenchmen, who called on him to stand or they would fire. He did what any man in his place would do; he surrendered, thanking God, no doubt, that his fate was no worse. Once more he was a prisoner, in what he calls 'this deplorably melancholy condition.' Apparently all were captured, their lives spared, and they were brought back in triumph to Miramichi.

Louisbourg fell before the genius of Wolfe on July 26, 1758; the news reached Miramichi on the second of August. The great outwork had fallen, and the road was now clear to the heart of New France. It must have been soon after, and on account of this disaster, that the prisoners were transferred to Quebec.

The first entries in the journal at Quebec tell the miseries of a prisoner's life. 'These cold walls' Witherspoon finds 'a poor place of abode.' The prison ration was scanty and almost uneatable. Money had little purchasing power. Even with the magnificent allowance of sevenpence ha'-penny 'starling' per diem, he found it hard living. In his own phrase, he can hardly 'rub and go.' Friends and messmates sicken and go off to the hospital where the sole treatment for all disorders is bleeding and physicking. Some return; but more do not. Prisoners are exchanged, but

Witherspoon continues in close confinement. Benevolent John Thompson of Boston lets the prisoners have money, or they would not be able to keep soul and body together, and takes letters to Witherspoon's wife and brother. Somehow or other, in spite of the bad food and scant allowance of firewood, Witherspoon managed to struggle through the long, tedious, bitterly cold winter. To his surprise, he finds that in spite of his privations his health is better. All his mess-mates have been in hospital; but he has escaped. In this mercy he sees the finger of God. Spring of the fateful year 1759 came sweet and early. The ice in the river broke up a month before the usual time. Our farmer notes the season as 'extraordinary good both for corn and grass as ever I think I saw it in New England both for showers and likewise sunshine—very temperate weather.'

On the twentieth of May, the crew of a Bristol brigantine captured off Cape Race by a French frigate brought the prisoners word that the campaign had opened. A British armada was on its way across the Atlantic. Six days later, they learn that

British ships are in the river. That is the whole entry for the date, as if no comment could enhance the value of such good news. The next entry ends with a prayer that God 'would be pleased to appear for us and direct our Admirals and Generals in this great affair whearin our Nation so much depends in a particular manner in North America.' The very prisoners in durance felt the significance of the oncoming struggle.

That the prisoners were on short allowance is little wonder. The investment of Quebec sent all food up to famine prices. 'I seed,' notes Witherspoon, 'six ounces of Bread sold hear in prison for 3s. 10d. sterling, brandy is 13s. 4d. per quart, and every other thing according to it.' Other prices he records are peas £2 10s. per bushel, bread 2s. 6d. per pound, which rose in September to 3s. and 3s. 6d. per pound. Milk, on which Witherspoon lived to avoid the sickening prison diet, cost fifteen sols per quart. Maple sugar was 8s. 9d. per pound and butter 5s. 3d. Once the prisoners paid two guineas for a calf, which weighed only twenty pounds. Townspeople and soldiers suffered as well as the prisoners. The prison doctor told the English captives he did not care how soon the country should be given up. He had nothing to give his wife and children. Witherspoon saw the troops killing for food the cats, as they ran about the town.

Miserable as was the prisoners' lot, worse was in store for them. The bombardment of the city from the new-made batteries at Levis threatened them with instant death. 'About 9 at night then our army began to throw in shells in great plenty, they fell round us on every corner which indeed was very awful,' runs the hasty entry, which tells of their deadly peril. No vivid imagination is needed to picture the terrors of that night. Nine men were crowded into a narrow cell with barely elbow room, listening to the roar of the cannonade, the shriek of the shell through the air and the crash of its explosion, 'on every corner,' and the still more dreadful intervals of silence. They must have suffered an agony of apprehension almost as bitter as death itself.

The tension they had undergone is shown clearly by the language of the journal next morning and the action they took. It was a day of excited angry conferences in the cell and of negotiations with their jailors. First they actually threaten to 'break out' if the governor 'did not provide a place of more safety' for them. At eleven o'clock, the town-major visits their cell and tells them that he has been to see Montcalm about effecting an exchange of prisoners. If this cannot be arranged, 'they would put us into a place of more safety.' At four in the afternoon, the town-major returned with the message that 'the General did not see fit to exchange at the present time . . . . he likewise told us that we must keep ourselves contented as they had no other place of safety.' Witherspoon's comment 'a most barbarous piece of cruelty' no doubt reflects but faintly the language of those desperate men. Their next proposal was to 'enter into b'onds' with the General for the removal of a few from the death-trap. Those who remained would 'suffer death,' if any of their more fortunate comrades broke parole. But they had little hope that their magnanimous petition would be granted; and, in fact, they all remained in their prison until the fall of Quebec.

Four days later, the city was again heavily bombarded. Two shells actually crashed through the roof of the barracks without, however, killing or wounding any of the prisoners. One of them was cool enough to keep tally, and he counted one hundred and five shot and shell fired into the city between eight o'clock in the evening and midnight, which Witherspoon considers 'in great plenty.'

On the 27th of July, the commissary of the army visited the men in prison at eleven o'clock, evidently for the purpose of reasoning with them about their situation. In the first place, there were no prisons in Quebec, such as were to be found in other parts of the world; and next, 'he did not look upon it as safe for us to desire . . . to be moved any distance out of the city . . . the Indians being about in great plenty they would surely kill us at a time as this when their blood was so hot.' At four, they received Montcalm's official reply to their petition, which was simply that he had no other place in which to put them. The Englishmen were furious. Old prisoners, who had seen the inside of Quebec dungeons before, declared that there were

other quarters, but they were reserved for
'their own people.' Witherspoon concludes
sadly, 'we have made all the interest that
possibly we can but all in vain.' These
negotiations with insignificant enemies
wholly in his power throw a sidelight on
the number and variety of Montcalm's con-
cerns that last summer of his life with the
fate of New France hanging in the balance.
Spurred on once more by the fear of death,
the prisoners drew up another petition to
the commissary the very next day, offering
hostages for their good behaviour. Witherspoon does not tell what became of it, but
he thanks God fervently, as well he might,
that he is still alive at the end of the week.

Apparently the prisoners had the freedom
of the barrack-yard and could see a great
deal that went on as they looked out over
that magnificent prospect which the modern tourist sees from Dufferin Terrace.
Witherspoon was a keenly interested eye-
witness of the English repulse at Montmor-
enci on the last day of July. About noon
he saw the *Centurion* and two armed
transports, which he calls 'frigets,' run in
close to the French shore-battery and engage hotly. The firing 'held all afternoon.'

The British intentions were quite clear to the eager spectator, who observes, 'Our army had a design by their actions to land that afternoon there being a vast number of boats cruising back and forth. About six in the evening the boats rowed close in with the shore which caused us to think they were going to land as we could see the whole acted from the prison but just as our army was about to land there came up a very great shower, whether this hindered them or not I cannot tell; but the Boats all moved off very soon.' Our Puritan is an honest man. He puts down just what he sees, and no more. Every reader of Parkman knows that the landing did take place and failed on account of that unlucky cloud-burst and the unsoldierly impetuosity of the grenadiers. In those few moments while Witherspoon was straining his eyes towards the smoke of the engagement, over four hundred brave fellows were struck down. This he could not know, or he would have been even more depressed by the sight of the blazing transports fired by the English in their slow and orderly retreat.

August passed without any other great

assault upon the city. The bombardment continued, and made Quebec a ruin; but Witherspoon could see, as well as Wolfe, how indecisive this operation must be. 'According to my weak judgment this scheme will never do; all they can do is only to beat down the houses, but this will not take the place, there being hardly any people in the city so that there is but very few lives lost.' One grim reality of war witnessed by this English captive was the execution of French deserters. He does not wonder at their desertion. Their living is very hard, the same as that of the prisoners, one pound of bread and half a pound of pork per day. 'Almost every day sees men executed for deserting from their colours. . . . and they give them but short time to consider of these things, some are taken one night and hanged the next day.' Apparently, the prisoners' request had been partially granted and they were transferred to some noisome underground vault. Their health suffered in consequence. Almost daily, some unfortunate was carried off to hospital. So they begged to be removed to their former quarters, bad as they were. 'We thought it safer to trust God for the event of what would happen than to lodge in such a place where our health was so much exposed.' Witherspoon thinks of his wife and children and praises God for the measure of health he still retains, 'when so many of my fellow mortals with pale faces are hanging about those walls.'

As the summer wore on towards the fateful thirteenth of September, coming events seemed to cast their shadows before. On the third of the month, all the prisoners were locked up, and the jailor gave them to understand that they 'expected the English would storm the town very soon.' Rumours flew about that if the siege lasted until the fifteenth, 'this place will be given up.' Some of the more free-spoken prisoners, 'ruffians,' Witherspoon calls them, insolently confident of British success, bragged that one of their guardians, Mr. Lorais, would be the first man they would strip. These 'brags' caused all the prisoners to be closely confined; but, by the eighth, they were free to walk 'in the yard as usual.' There was a lull before the great battle.

On the very day, Witherspoon had more than an inkling of what actually took place. 'About 5 in the morning they began up above the town to fire pretty smartly, at what distance I cannot say for we could only hear the report of their guns; about ten the battle began very smart with a continual fire which held till after 12, by which I cannot but think there is a considerable number on both sides gone into eternity. But by what I could learn our army got the better of it . . . . by the report of their arms they seemed to be drove close home to the city to us, and the French on all hands looking very melancholy.' He is fairly accurate in his time and in his inferences. It is easy to picture the wakeful men in their narrow cell consulting, conjecturing, listening to the crackle and roar of the musketry fire coming nearer and nearer, and watching the French faces to read the news there. On the next day, the prisoners are again confined to their rooms. The French are blowing up their batteries to the north of the city, 'our fleet and army having them hemmed in now on every quarter.' Witherspoon has hope that with the blessing of God 'this affair will soon come to an end.' He sees the poor breeding mothers carrying one child and leading another by the hand. It is a

melancholy sight and arouses his sympathy
for 'their trouble and difficulties.'

Late on the fifteenth, our diarist gets the
news that was to set the bells ringing in
Boston and London, the decisive victory of
the Plains of Abraham on the 13th. He
sees the French issuing new clothing to
their troops; but hears little or no firing.
'A little before night there was another
prisoner brought in that was taken the day
the battle was fought. He gave us some
account of how the battle went. He told
us that General Wolfe was killed, which I
am very sorry to hear and so ought every
one of us to be . . . to reflect upon the
great loss, such an excellent man for war
as General Wolf was. Who by the report
I have heard of him by the soldiers, they
all give him excellent . . .' How that
nameless soldier must have been mobbed
by the white-faced, eager prisoners! It is
noteworthy that he tells of Wolfe's death
before he tells of his victory. Witherspoon
adds his testimony to Wolfe's popularity in
the army.

'He likewise told us that General
Montcalm was killed and their Governor
and Lieutenant Governor with 24 more

of their officers were taken prisoners,
and they judged 500 of the French
killed and a great many taken prisoners.
The battle began early in the morning,
our army drove the enemy above
four miles before the hight of the battle
began.' Unfortunately here occur gaps in
the manuscript; the last pages would be
frayed and blurred. Witherspoon learns
that the final scene was 'not above a mile
from the city,' which is correct, and that
'it was as dreadful a battle as ever was
fought in North America . . . after the fire
the Granadeers and highlanders ran in upon
them and cut them down in great numbers.'
This, one of the very earliest accounts of
the battle, is strangely accurate in the main
points. What impressed Witherspoon most
was the death of Wolfe; he comes back to
this theme several times, recording the
number of Wolfe's wounds and the fact
that he and his great rival have fallen together. The next day he writes his epitaph: ' . . . whose soul I hope and trust
is now in Heaven, who has died like a brave
soldier in the defence of his king and country.'

On the nineteenth the prison doors

opened at last on freedom, and the journal ends with the entry for that day. Witherspoon must have remained in the city until the spring, with still more hardships to endure; but, in the end, he returned safe to his wife and children and to his farm in the valley of the Annapolis. Later records mention him as a man of substance, the head of a household of eight persons, and the owner of two oxen, three cows, three young cattle, and two swine. It is not likely that he ever forgot his captivity among the French and Indians, and least of all the cold, the sickness, the starvation in the barracks of Quebec. There the lot of prisoners seems to have been notoriously severe. A scrap of old ballad handed down by family tradition runs thus:

> And poor prisoners, we'll release.
> And the last words General Wolfe said
> Were, 'Brave boys, I die in peace.'

IV

Trials of a Sympathizer

IV

Trials of a Sympathizer

ALIFAX, the ancient and picturesque capital of Nova Scotia,
is visited every summer by hundreds of American tourists.
They enjoy their escape from the torrid
heats of August at home to the cool sea
air, the clear blue days, and the peaceful,
sleep-filled nights, and they find no little
interest in the bowery public gardens, the
mazes of the sea-girt park, the royal prospects from the star-shaped citadel, and the
many monuments that record the history of
this old garrison town. As long ago as the
eighteenth century, during the American
Revolution, hundreds of American citizens
used to visit the place, but they did not
come willingly; they were singularly blind
to its scenic charm and they took the earliest possible opportunity of returning to
their native land. They were, in fact,
prisoners of war gathered up by His Bri-

tannic Majesty's cruisers and land forces. They were confined in jails and prison-ships and barracks, and they lived on prisoner's fare. Their lot was hard and they gave the city of their captivity a bad name which it was slow to shake off. Sooner or later, they were sent home by cartel, in exchange for British prisoners gathered up by the Continentals; but the more impatient broke out by force or stratagem, and the sympathizing Nova Scotians helped them 'up along to the west-ward' on their way to freedom. The rape of the *Flying Fish* is a case in point; and the story shows how peaceful men suffer in time of war.

On the evening of April 7, 1780, a little ten ton schooner with this poetic name lay at a wharf in Halifax, probably Fairbanks', near the foot of Blowers street. With the help of a single other hand, William Green-wood had brought her up from Barrington, a small fishing-village at the butt-end of the province, to the capital, with a load of potatoes. He had sold his cargo, possibly to the commissariat department, for Hali-fax had a huge garrison to feed at the time; and he had received his money. He had also his clearance from the Customs and he was ready to sail. Between eight and nine o'clock he was in the tiny cabin with the other man, the two forming the entire crew; he may have been getting ready to turn in for the night, or he may have been reckoning up the profits of the trip, or considering how soon he could get back to Barrington and begin the spring fishing. He had on board nets and other gear, and he knew where he could procure a sufficiency of salt; he may have been thinking of the Banks. Or he may have been meditating on the varied experiences of the past five years, since the Thirteen Colonies had declared their independence of the mother country.

The war had been a hard trial for poor men like William Greenwood. Only ten years before it broke out, he had left his native state of Massachusetts for Nova Scotia and had settled at Barrington for greater convenience to the rich fisheries of the North Atlantic. He was a British subject. He had simply transferred himself and his belongings from one British colony to another, and now, for no fault of his, by the ironic accident of mere residence, he

found himself an enemy to his old friends
and the kindred he had left behind. How
could he be expected to bear arms against
them? How could he help sympathizing
with the 'rebels,' against whom the governor and Assembly of Nova Scotia fulmin-
ated in menacing Acts and proclamations?
It was a cruel situation for a poor man, especially after Congress had declared that
the Thirteen Colonies would have no trade
or commerce with the two erring sisters to
the north, which had refused to join the
union. The fishermen of Barrington and
Yarmouth soon felt the pinch of want.
Fishing was their sole means of livelihood;
to move back to Massachusetts meant ruin;
to remain in Nova Scotia exposed them to
the American privateers and shut them out
from their natural market.

Still, men are not as harsh as their laws;
even in the worst year of the war, commerce
between Nova Scotia and Massachusetts
did not wholly cease. In October, 1776,
the Barrington men loaded the schooner
Hope with fish and liver oil and sent her
to Salem with a piteous request that they
might be allowed to barter the cargo for
provisions, to keep them through the long

winter approaching. It is impossible, they said, to get provisions elsewhere. The homely petition breaks into an irrepressible cry of distress—'God only knows what will become of us.' To resist such an appeal was not easy. The House of Representatives allowed the agent of the *Hope,* Heman Kenney, to dispose of his cargo, and to purchase two hundred and fifty bushels of corn, thirty barrels of pork, two hogsheads of molasses, two hogsheads of rum (a necessity of life), and two hundred pounds of coffee. With these rations, rather plentiful and luxurious compared with what they purchased in later years, the community at Barrington managed somehow or other to get through the long winter.

Exactly a year later, Greenwood had been able to render an important service to the new republic by restoring to it no fewer than twenty-five of its fighting men. Captain Littlefield Libby had the misfortune to lose his privateer. She was driven on shore by one of H.B.M.'s cutters. Her crew set her on fire and took to the woods. After a toilsome journey of seventeen leagues through the primeval forest, they reached

Barrington and bought a boat with what money they had, eked out with their shoe-buckles and thirty small-arms. But ill luck still followed them. They were wrecked and lost their dear bought boat. Once more they were forced back on the limited hospitality of the fishing hamlet at the east passage of Cape Sable Island. In this crisis, Greenwood undertook to ferry them over in his forty-five ton schooner, the *Sally,* which may have been named after his wife. In addition to Libby's crew, he brought one of Captain Fullerby's men and three others who had escaped from Halifax and had made their way to the end of the province nearest their own home. The plan of the previous year was repeated. On Captain Libby's advice, the *Sally* was loaded with a few quintals of fish, the result of the labour of many families, some bushels of salt, and some fish-oil to be exchanged for corn, or wheaten flour, for the indispensable daily bread. By October 27, 1777, the *Sally* with her cargo and her returning privateersmen was safe at Salem, and, four days later, Greenwood's petition for leave to buy food was granted.

For the return trip, Greenwood had

shipped a new hand, one John Caldwell, a young fisherman, whose artless tale illustrates the sufferings of the innocent noncomb'atants in time of war. He lived in Nova Scotia, not far from Barrington, where the visionary Colonel Alexander McNutt projected his marvellous city of New Jerusalem. Caldwell was the only support of his widowed mother and his sisters. The fishery had been ruined by the depredations of the merciless small privateers, so he made a voyage in a merchantman from Nova Scotia to the West Indies. On his return, he avers that he was 'strongly importun'd' to go on another voyage to Quebec; so he must have been a likely lad. On his way thither, his vessel was snapped up by the privateer *Dolphin* out of Salem, and he himself was made prisoner of war. Now he petitioned for release, and the Council of Massachusetts were not without bowels. They considered his motives, his youth, and his peculiar circumstances, as he requested, and they gave him leave to return in the *Sally* to his own place.

The next October saw Greenwood again in Boston with his annual cargo of escaping prisoners on board the *Sally,* and his annual petition for leave to buy food. His passenger list included Amos Green of Salem, Ichabod Mattocks of Mount Desert, and Mr. John Long, late quartermaster of the Continental ship *Hancock.* She had been captured by that very active officer Sir George Collier of the *Rainbow* in a sea duel, like that between the *Chesapeake* and the *Shannon,* and taken to Halifax. The local jail must have been a curious place. The jailor was infirm and delegated his duties to his wife. The supply of shackles was insufficient and the regulations for visiting the prisoners at night were not enforced. Apparently nobody with any contrivance remained long in durance. Americans were always escaping and always being helped 'up along' by the people of Nova Scotia.

So far Greenwood, the 'hearty friend of America,' as Captain Libby calls him, had managed to escape being ground between the upper and nether millstones of the hostile forces, but soon he was to suffer not from 'the enemy,' but from the Americans whom he had consistently befriended.

Early on the morning of the twentieth

of August, 1779, the fishing hamlet at Ragged Islands was surprised by American privateersmen from Coaxset. They had made the journey of four hundred miles in three open whale-boats. After setting a guard on the house, 'they went a-robing,' as the injured ones testified. Nineteen quintals of codfish, four barrels of salt, three salmon nets, sixty pounds of butter, one green hide, six dressed skins, and some cheese were part of the loot. The people of Ragged Islands felt aggrieved. They had helped three or four hundred prisoners 'up along to America,' and had concealed privateers and even prizes from the British cruisers. After sacking Ragged Islands, the whalers went to Barrington and despoiled Greenwood of the faithful *Sally*. He followed up the robbers, but it does not appear that he ever secured redress.

In September of the same year, this humble American patriot was loading a vessel at Barrington with the property of Mr. John Pitts of Boston, when an armed boat from Rhode Island entered the harbour, cut the vessels adrift and proceeded to rifle the store-house of Mr. John Pitts' valuable goods. In consequence of this outrage, Greenwood did not get to Boston until December. In that month, thanks to the protection of the great Mr. Pitts, he obtained permission to purchase twenty-five bushels of rye and twenty-five bushels of Indian corn for the support of his family (he was a married man with young children) and of other distressed persons at Barrington. He also obtained a 'protection' against American armed vessels, and he seems to have intended returning, bag and baggage, to his native state of Massachusetts in the following spring. He had brought his vessel across single-handed, but now he asked for the loan of a boy out of the prison-ship at Boston to help him work her back to Barrington. He promised to return a person, that is, an escaping American, in exchange for the borrowed hand.

In the spring, he was at Halifax, instead of home in Massachusetts, a fact that was afterwards used against him. The potatoes, which he and, no doubt, other thrifty fishermen had raised and kept through the winter, were surplus stock and specially valuable as being out of season. His reasons for trading with 'the enemy' were obvious. Oppressive Britain paid, not in depreciated paper, but in good solid gold and silver. Besides, those 'moving things called wife and weans' would lead him to bring his goods to the best, nearest, and safest market. History now finds William Greenwood at a definite place and date with all this experience behind him.

Whatever may have been passing through his mind, as he sat with his mate in the cramped cabin of the *Flying Fish* that April night, he could hardly have had any inkling that he was on the eve of his greatest and most unpleasant adventure. He could not know that on the wharf outside in the darkness six grimy, desperate American soldiers were scrutinizing the little schooner with anxious eyes, and, in stealthy whispers were planning her capture. They were Thomas Hooper of Beverley, William Forbes (or Forbush) of Salem, one Jarvis, one Jenks, and a Scot whose name does not transpire. The sixth, their leader, called himself James Reed, but the name he gave in his affidavit was William Stanton. He had been swept up by 'the enemy' at Stony Point on the Hudson, and, as that post was carried by the Americans under Wayne on July 15, 1779, he must have been captured prior to that date. They had all been confined for 'some months' in Halifax and that very hour, between eight and nine, they had succeeded in digging a tunnel out under the jail, and now they were looking for a vessel in which to escape. They were still in great danger. The place swarmed with redcoats. The main guard was next the jail. Patrols, sentries, batteries were everywhere. If they did not escape by water, they were sure to be discovered and haled back to prison. Now, by the greatest good luck, they stumbled on the man and the vessel in Halifax most likely that night to complete their rescue.

But they knew nothing of Greenwood, his disposition, or his sympathies. Their first step was to discover, if possible, how many hands were on board. Stanton undertook to find out. Stripping off his own shirt, or procuring one of his comrades he went on board boldly, entered the cabin and offered it for sale. His action was not surprising. In those days when factories were unknown and sewing-machines not invented, a linen shirt was a rare piece of

needlework with a distinct market value.
Soldiers and sailors were continually sell-
ing their 'slops' for the price of a few drinks.
The practice was forbidden by Nova Scotia
law. While Stanton was engaging Greenwood's attention, Hooper followed him
down the companion-way, also with an article to sell—this time, a razor. As the
two conspirators were chaffering below, the
other four silently cast off, and took possession of the deck. The *Flying Fish* began
to drift out into the harbour and soon the
sound of water lapping overside apprised
Stanton and Hooper of their comrades'
success. At once they drew their bayonets (why or how prisoners of war should
have been allowed to retain their side-arms
is not explained) and told Greenwood and
his mate that if they dared to resist they
were dead men.

Taken completely by surprise, the lawful owners made no fight, and a parley en-
sued. The violent strangers soon made it
clear that they were American soldiers
trying to escape. Indeed, though ragged
and dirty, they were still in the buff and
blue uniform of the Continental Army.
Greenwood, hearty friend of America as he

was, knew that in helping them he was
risking his neck. He represented how dangerous it was 'for him to carry away Soldiers (they being all dressed in Regimen-
tals) as he must expect to suffer for it if
he was Catched.' 'Suffer' meant, of
course, 'stretching hemp.' One of them
replied he would kill or be killed, and
Greenwood had no choice but submission.
About nine o'clock the sails were hoisted,
and Greenwood took the helm. Stanton
and Hooper stood guard on each side with
their bayonets threatening instant death if
he tried to run the schooner aground in the
darkness or to speak so loud as to be heard
on shore. In such guise, the lightless *Flying Fish* slipped down the harbour before
the north wind between McLean's Battery
on the starboard hand and George's to port,
past all the works on Point Pleasant, past
Sandwich Point and Thrum Cap, unchallenged, to the open sea and safety. Sel-
dom, indeed, has fickle Fortune so signally
favoured daring and desperate men. Within an hour of digging themselves out of
prison, they had captured a vessel and were
bowling along straight for home and freedom.

Squint suspicion always clings to an alias. That the same man should call himself at one time James Reed, and, at another, William Stanton clouds all his narrative with a doubt, but this is the tale he told 'repeatedly' in the presence of Rachel Chandler and Mary Hambleton of North Yarmouth, on Great Chebeag Island. His five comrades heard his repeated story and agreed in the details. The sworn testimony of the two ladies is confirmed by the affidavit of Jacob Curtis of Great Chebeag and by Greenwood's petition. Stanton seems to have been a talkative person, and, therefore, apt to say more than he knew. In his affidavit, he poses as Greenwood's friend by minimizing the violence used in seizing his schooner and tells chiefly what took place after they were clear of Halifax.

According to his account, nothing of importance occurred until the *Flying Fish* had flown some thirty marine leagues 'up along to the westward.' She would do at least her five or six knots an hour; therefore, it was probably the next afternoon that Greenwood steered her into an unnamed harb'our, which must have been at Ragged Islands, that nest of American sym-

pathizers. Still he ran no risks. Stanton
swears that he 'took every prudent measure
to prevent our being discovered . . . He
went on shore while our vessel lay aground
and never discovered us to the inhabitants.'
Stanton believed that 'the said Greenwood
might have taken said schooner from us if
he had been so minded.' It seems plain
that if Greenwood was at first intimidated
into carrying these prisoners away, he was
now willing to help them to the utmost of
his power, which is thoroughly consistent
with his conduct all through the war.

What happened next day was sheer outrage. Early on the morning of April 9,
the *Flying Fish* was once more under way,
still heading westward. When she had
run some five leagues, a shallop came within hail. It belonged to Greenwood's
brother, who was on board with three
other men. Greenwood sent his passengers
below on the ballast that they might not be
recognized. He sailed about two leagues
farther. Then that voyage ended abruptly for him and the single 'hand.'

It seems the chance meeting of the
two Greenwoods aroused the soldiers' suspicions. Stanton tells that he was sum-

moned on deck by 'four of our company
. . . . They told me they had agreed to
set Greenwood ashore on a desolate
island.' Stanton would not consent, but
the four insisted on marooning or killing
Greenwood. That luckless person, now
a quasi-prisoner in his own cabin, offered
to take them to Salem, if they would
allow him to land his chest and the one man
who composed his crew. At first they
agreed to this proposal, but soon they
changed their minds. Stanton acted as a
go-between and peacemaker, and showed
his friends Greenwood's 'protection' obtained from the Massachusetts Council the
year before. From this document they
gathered that they could not make the
Flying Fish lawful prize; and, once more,
they were all for killing Greenwood and his
man. According to Stanton, he begged
their lives, and the others agreed to spare
them if they would go ashore peaceably.
'On which I went into the cabin and gave
him to understand there was a plot and
made signs for him to go on shore.' Greenwood's next and natural request was to be
set ashore with his sea-chest, containing, no
doubt, all his property. He would make

shift to get it home. But they would not listen to him. They demanded his money 'with a cocked pistol at his breast,' stripped him 'of all his clothes' and put him and his man ashore on the nearest 'desolate island,' which must have been Negro Island, and made off with the schooner. Greenwood's sole epithet for their conduct is 'ungrateful.'

Probably he did not remain long marooned on Negro Island. He was only some seven miles from his home, and, if his brother was cruising in the neighbourhood, he may have been taken off the same day. How the six soldiers managed to navigate the stolen *Flying Fish* is not recorded, but Yankee ingenuity would be equal to the task. Forbush as a Salem man must have been half a sailor. At any rate, their wonderful luck still held, for they brought their prize safely into Casco Bay. There they sold her to Daniel Wyer, mariner, Nathan Bucknam, yeoman, David Chandler, and Reuben Noble for five thousand (depreciated) dollars. The adventurers lived in different parts of the continent, they were eager to reach their homes, and they needed the money for travelling expenses. Evidently they shared the proceeds of the sale and separated, each to his own place.

On their way to Casco, Stanton told his friends that Greenwood would recover his vessel. The idea was not well received. Thomas Hooper of Beverley and William Forbush of Salem were particularly truculent. If Greenwood came to Salem, or Boston, or Marblehead on any such errand, they would 'knock him on the head and throw him over the wharf,' phrases that bear the impress of reality. None the less Stanton was a true prophet. By the end of April, Greenwood was in Boston petitioning the Council for the recovery of his vessel. He had powerful friends and he had deserved well of the republic.

On the second of May the House of Representatives appointed a committee of two, General Warren and Major Cross, to look into the matter. To their number was added the powerful Mr. John Pitts, who knew all about the petitioner and had himself suffered in pocket from his own side in the war. This committee acted with great promptitude, for the very next day the prayer of the petition was granted as far as possible. The local Committee of

Correspondence was empowered to take possession of the *Flying Fish,* pending the action of the General Court, and to serve the present owners with copies of Greenwood's petition, and the order of the court 'to show cause if any they have' why they should keep what did not belong to them.

Naturally 'the present owners,' Nathan Bucknam, mariner, and his friends, who had bought and paid for Greenwood's schooner, objected vigorously to surrendering her. They filed a counter-petition, emphasizing the fact that the schooner had been taken by force and was therefore a lawful prize. They tried to make it appear that Greenwood was a dubious character, who wanted to run with the hare and hunt with the hounds. That in his clearance, the shallop was called the *Peggy,* that he had gone to Halifax instead of Massachusetts in the spring, that 'the enemy was prob'ably supplied' with his cargo of potatoes,—all these things were twisted into suspicious circumstances. But they made up no case. Justice prevailed, and, by the middle of June, Greenwood had his property restored and was on his way back to Barrington.

History vouchsafes one more glimpse of

him. On August 2, 1782, he sailed from Barrington in a small schooner with a hundred quintals of fish, the property of some thirty poor families of that place. He had on board six escaped prisoners. Five were privateersmen of the schooner *Fox* out of Newburyport. One of these, Zebulon Rowe, was 'of lawful age,' and his testimony has been preserved. He had started on a short-lived cruise against 'the enemies of the United States of America . . . On the second day after we sailed from Georges River we were captured by the British frigate *Ceres,* carried into Halifax and there confined on board the prison-ship.' About the 20th of July, Zebulon and his four shipmates made their escape, and 'with much difficulty arrived at Barrington in Nova Scotia without money or provisions.' Here they found Greenwood, the leading man of the village, 'who kindly supplied us with whatever we needed, gratis . . . . We applied to the said Greenwood to bring us to Newburyport, but it was with the greatest difficulty that we prevailed with him to consent to bring us, as he had lately lost his wife and had nobody but a girl to leave a family of small children with, and was just engaged in his mowing.' So Mrs. Greenwood, poor soul, had her own troubles, the woman's part, in these calamitous years. Greenwood had his private grief, his motherless children, and the inexorable labour of the earth to tie him to his home, but he listened to the call of humanity. He loaded his schooner with all the fish the hamlet had ready and carried it, with Zebulon Rowe, and the other 'Foxes' safe to Newburyport. 'He never charged us a farthing for his trouble or our provisions,' says the grateful privateersman. And then,—the naval officer of the port obeyed the letter of the law forbidding all intercourse with Nova Scotia, and seized both vessel and cargo.

Finally Greenwood got his schooner back and obtained permission to exchange the hundred quintals of fish for such necessaries and articles as the naval officer, Mr. Michael Hodge, might think proper. He was further ordered by the Commonwealth of Massachusetts to pay any expenses zealous Mr. Hodge might have incurred in the discharge of his duty. So he is out of the saga, and returns to his darkened home, his mowing, and his fishing. A hamlet in

Nova Scotia bears his name, and his descendants are to be found where he lived and suffered more than a century ago.

V

Tonge at Petit de Grat

V

Tonge at Petit de Grat

N the eastern coast of Cape Breton lie two small islands called Isle Madame and Petit de Grat, familiar to all sea-captains as 'Peter the Great.' The narrow inlet between them was the scene of a fight which deserves to be remembered, because the victory went to the weaker side. It was courage, skill, and resolution pitted against long odds; and, for once, Providence was not on the side of the big battalions.

In the year 1781, France had come actively to the support of the revolted British colonies in America. From the first, she had supplied Washington with the munitions of war, and now French sailors and soldiers were fighting, like the colonists themselves, for American independence. It was the French fleet which compelled Cornwallis to surrender at Yorktown. All through the conflict, little Nova Scotia stood by the mother country with unshaken loyalty, and the province suffered in consequence. Its coasts were constantly harried by the enemy's privateers; and various settlements were sacked by landing parties from the ships.

On the 21st of July, 1781, two fine French frigates of the largest class were cruising in company off Cape Breton, about six sea leagues south-east of Cape North, not far from Spanish River, where the busy steel city of Sydney now stands. They were notable ships. The *Astrée,* of forty-four guns, was commanded by the famous explorer La Pérouse, who captured Fort Prince of Wales on Hudson's Bay, and who was destined, like Captain Cook, to find death in the islands of the Pacific. Her sister ship, the *Hermione* of forty-two guns, had for captain Latouche-Tréville, who became Napoleon's favourite admiral. Nelson once swore, if he caught him, to make him eat a lying gazette he issued. His name is borne by a French battleship of the present day.

About nine o'clock in the morning, the French ships sighted some twenty sail rounding the island of Scattarie. It was a small squadron of unarmed sloops and schooners bound to Spanish River for coal, to keep the huge garrison at Halifax warm in the coming winter. With them were four provision ships loaded with flour and salt, which had lain in Halifax harbour since the St. Lawrence became ice-bound the year before. They were urgently needed at Quebec, and Governor Haldimand had dispatched the provincial armed ship *Jack* under Captain Richard Peter Tonge from that city on the twelfth of June, with orders to proceed to Halifax and bring back the over-due victuallers.

Tonge was a zealous and capable officer. He had come out from London as first mate in the Treasury brig *Mary* at the beginning of the war, and had served with distinction on the River Richelieu, in Lake Ontario, and in the Gulf. The year before, he had recaptured the provincial armed schooner *Mercury* (in the provincial armed brig *Polly*). His chief, Schanks, thought well of him and recommended him to Haldimand. His new command, the *Jack,* was a tiny full-rigged ship of 160 tons, mounting ten 9-pounders and four sixes.

On the way down, the *Jack* had met

9

with a serious accident. While off Seal Island, two days after leaving Quebec, she encountered 'a most severe gust of wind at S. W. attended with much Thunder and Lightning, which broke right over us,' as the captain reports. It took the mizzen-mast off short about fifteen feet above the deck, without in the least injuring the top-mast or the rigging. The broken mast fell 'almost perpendicularly' and three sailors were injured thereby. Next day about the same time, the crippled *Jack* made Bic; and, in three hours and a half, the energetic crew had selected, cut, and brought to the ship another mast from the woods three miles away. Six hours later, they had the new mast stepped and rigged, and were ready to proceed. They did that sort of thing in the old navy.

The flag-ship of the convoy was the cap-tured 'rebel' frigate *Boston,* renamed the *Charlestown* in honor of a notable Brit-ish victory, better known to the world as the battle of Bunker Hill. She mounted twenty-eight guns, and was commanded by a very active officer named Henry Francis Evans, who was well liked in Halifax, whither he had sent many prizes. Two others were sloops-of-war, that is, three-masted, square-rigged vessels of a class below the frigate; these were the *Allegiance* and the *Vulture,* with seven guns a side. The latter carried men of the 70th regiment, who had been detailed to dig coal, and who now waited with fixed bayonets for an opportunity to board, which never came. 'Vulture' might be thought a name of ill omen. In September, 1780, this same sloop-of-war carried Major John André up the Hudson to West Point in order to complete arrangements for betraying this key position to the British. It was to this same *Vulture* that Benedict Arnold fled on the morning of September 25, when his treason was discovered; it was from the *Vulture* that he wrote his famous letter to Washington, exculpating his beautiful wife—'she is as good and innocent as an angel.' The fifth vessel was the armed provincial ship *Vernon,* named no doubt in honor of 'Old Grog,' who took Porto Bello with six ships only. All together, the five English vessels were not a match for the two Frenchmen in size of crew and weight of metal.

That twenty-first of July, the last day of

his life, must have been full of anxiety to
Captain Evans. After reconnoitring the
strangers and finding that they could not
answer his signals, his great care was to
get his convoy safe to port. Wind and
weather conditions favoured him. The
French frigates had to beat up against
light summer airs, while the colliers and
victuallers coasted close-hauled near the
shore. The English war-ships kept between the enemy and his prey until evening. There was some very fine seamanship on the part of Evans. Then about
seven o'clock, when the last sail of the convoy had disappeared into Spanish River,
he ranged his five vessels in line ahead and
awaited the attack of La Pérouse. It was
like five terriers fighting two mastiffs.

The battle began about seven o'clock,
and the last shot was fired about eight.
Within that hour sixty-two British sailors
and forty-two Frenchmen had been struck
down, killed or wounded. More than half
the British loss occurred on the deck of
the *Charlestown,* which shows that she
bore the brunt of the conflict. Gallant
Evans was killed by a cannon shot some
time after the action began, but the battle

was continued with the greatest coolness
and courage by his first officer, Mackay,
under the direction of Captain George of
the *Vulture*. All the English ships were
badly mauled. The *Jack* was forced to
strike her flag, after losing only three men.
The *Charlestown* had her main-top-mast
shot away and was almost helpless. The
French say that she too lowered her colours; but the night was pitch dark and the
matter is uncertain. In the morning the
enemies were far apart. The *Allegiance*
made Spanish River; and the other British
ships, badly shattered, returned to Halifax.
Captain Evans was given a splendid funeral. He was buried beneath historic St.
Paul's, where a mural tablet still preserves
his name and the memory of his last fight.

The *Astrée* was so damaged in her rigging that she could not pursue. Squalls
in the night drove her and her consort far
to the westward; but finally they made
their way to Boston with their single prize.
The French naval historians represent La
Pérouse as fighting against heavy odds and
gaining a victory. A French marine artist,
the Marquis de Rossel, painted a picture of
the engagement, with the *Jack* surrender-

ing; it was one of a series of eighteen French naval victories painted by the order of the King of France, and it was engraved by Deguevauviller in 1790. The truth is that it was a drawn battle.

Why did the *Jack* surrender? Tonge was not that sort of man. In those days, fighting captains went into action with their flag nailed to the mast, so that it could not be lowered. The *Jack* lost only three men, which shows that she was not fought very long. One of them however was James Gormory, the man at the helm. If he was struck down, it was quite possible that the *Jack* engaging at close quarters would get out of hand, fall helplessly under the guns of the enemy, and have to choose between surrender and being blown out of the water. The killing of the steersman of the *Czarevitch* decided the fate of the Russian fleet in the battle of Tsushima. At all events, Tonge and his crew went to Boston as prisoners, and the *Jack* was sold to Salem as a prize. Next year, she was retaken at the mouth of Halifax harbour by the *Observer* privateer, Captain Crymes, after a desperate fight of two hours, in which the

Americans lost twenty-one officers and men out of a total crew of fifty-eight.

But Captain Tonge's adventures were only beginning. On the twenty-eighth of July, he was brought back to Halifax in a cartel, an exchanged prisoner with twenty-one of his crew. Naturally he was eager to return to his station at the earliest moment. No ship was ready to sail; navigation of the St. Lawrence would soon close. What was he to do? He was able to induce Brigadier-General John Campbell to buy at public auction the prize privateer *Greyhound* of six guns, out of Portsmouth, New Hampshire, which had been captured some thirty leagues to the westward of Halifax by H.M.S. *Assurance* on the twentieth of the month. Her hull cost £230; and more than eighty pounds additional were needed for her cable, cordage, a bolt of canvas, a new topmast, and other oddments, to fit her out. Two pounds ten went to the purchase of a new blue ensign from John Robertson, which was not to be disgraced. Finally, she was re-christened the *Little Jack,* a form of dear diminutive not uncommon among ships in those days. It cannot be fanciful to read in this title the sailor's affection for his floating home, and an allusion to the vessel he had lost.

By the fifth of Octob'er, the *Little Jack* was ready for sea, and the next day Tonge and his twenty-one set sail for Queb'ec. Four days after leaving Halifax, Tonge made the eastern entrance of the Gut of Canso, the strait which separates the peninsula of Nova Scotia from the island of Cape Breton. It is a narrow and picturesque passage with sheer cliffs rising abruptly from the water's edge almost like the mouth of the Saguenay. As he was entering, he met with a most unpleasant surprise. Coming out were two 'rebel' privateer schooners from Marblehead. The larger one was the *Hope,* of eighty tons, Richard Wormster, master, mounting eight four-pounders, though pierced for ten. Her sister ship was armed with eight swivels and one three-pounder. The odds were too great for battle. Tonge altered his course and ran for it. There was nothing else to do.

The entrance to the strait was barred; so the cutter fled eastward. The chase did not continue long. Either the *Little Jack* was overhauled too rapidly for any hope of escape, or else her captain changed his mind and formed, as he ran, a desperate plan of fighting. His mental processes are conjectural; but they may be judged by what actually happened.

Petit de Grat inlet is only twelve miles from the entrance to the Gut of Canso, and into this narrow defile Tonge steered the *Little Jack*. He may have thought he could get through, and then found that he could not; or he may have fancied that the Marbleheaders would not follow him into an unknown, dangerous channel. But the Americans were skilful and daring sailors; and where he went, they went. So Tonge prepared to fight. The measures he took show plainly that he was determined not to haul down his new blue ensign, as long as a stick would stand on board the *Little Jack*.

First, he anchored the cutter and brought a spring upon his cable. This means that a second rope was made fast to the anchor when it was dropped, and this 'spring line' was carried to the stern of the vessel. By 'heaving on the spring' the *Little Jack* was then warped round until her deadly battery of three guns (each perhaps carrying a four-pound shot) could rake the channel. In all likelihood, she took up a position somewhere near the site of the present lighthouse, where the channel narrows. The 'rebel' privateers must attack in single file. It was like following a bear into its cave.

Then the fight began. As soon as the Marbleheaders came within extreme range, the *Little Jack's* pop-guns began to bark. They recoiled in their breechings, and were reloaded, and were run out again. The Americans replied as their guns bore. The narrow strait—it is only two hundred yards wide—was filled with black powder smoke, and reverberated to the explosions of the cannon.

How long the fight lasted is not on record; but probably it did not last very long. The Americans pounded and Tonge pounded, but Tonge pounded longest. As the *Hope* led the way in and worked up the tortuous channel, a lucky shot from the *Little Jack* cut her fore-tie, which naturally brought down her foresail. Swiftly the resourceful Yankees knotted it and rehoisted the sail. But a second well-aimed shot carried it away again; to do the same trick twice means good gunnery. The *Hope* missed stays, and ran helplessly on a rock at extreme range, where the British guns could do no execution. The *Little Jack's* fire had been directed at the masts and rigging of the enemy in the hope of crippling them before they could close. It had been successful in attaining its object; but the Americans were very far from b'eing defeated. They were still in overwhelming force: their guns outranged the British: and they could smother Tonge and his little crew with boarders, even if they did not succeed in knocking the *Little Jack* into matchwood with their heavier metal. Then Tonge did a striking and original thing which shows the resource of the born fighter. While under fire he landed a gun. Where it came from is something of a mystery. As this piece of ordnance was a nine-pounder, it is highly improbable that it formed part of the cutter's own armament. She could not possibly carry six nine-pounders on her tiny deck. Such a heavy gun was probably in her hold being conveyed with its carriage, tackle, and ammunition to Quebec. Now, in the crisis of this uncertain fight, it was sweated out from below and over the side into the boat, and landed, and man-hauled up a rocky eminence near by. As it could not have weighed less than half a ton, the magnitude of the British sailors' task must be apparent. But landed it was. The exact position of the 'eminence' it crowned cannot be decided. All the coast is bleak and bare: and near the present light-house rises a knob of rock about a hundred and forty feet above the level of the sea. From this height, Tonge could obtain a plunging fire upon the defenceless decks of his enemies. It was a brilliant move in a game that seemed lost, and it proved to be the winning move.

There must have been no time to spare. The minutes must have been crowded with back-breaking toil and deep-sea language. But as soon as the big gun was in position with its carriage, quoins, tackle, hand-spikes, cartridge, and round-shot, the fortunes of the day changed. From the hill, a brisk cannonade was opened at once on the stationary target of the grounded *Hope,* cutting up her sails and rigging. No matter how brave the Americans were, they could make no effective reply, and when a nine-pound shot plumped through their main-mast close to the partners, they hauled down the 'rebel' flag.

That was the end of this gallant little fight. After the surrender of the *Hope,* the fire of the nine-pounder drove her consort out to sea. Tonge took possession of his big prize, and released all his prisoners on parole but one, to preserve as a specimen, I suppose. His handy men spent two days in repairing the damage they had done to the schooner's sails and rigging, and in fishing her wounded mainmast; but, by Friday the 12th of October, they had all a-taunto, and the two vessels proceeded in company to Quebec, reporting with a flourish of triumph, 'All well on board!' There the privateer was sold for £103. 14. 6. Tonge's share of the prize-money was £25. 18. 7½, which was something in those hard times.

Poor Tonge! He and his brave fight are both forgotten. After the war, he returned to London, where the latest records tell of a most pitiable fate. His wife died after a long illness, leaving him with three little children, homeless and penniless.

The authorities delayed granting him his half-pay, and refused him permission to join the Russian navy. 'If relief is not granted,' runs his latest petition, 'a Prison must be his portion and his Children of course abandoned.'

At the Harbour Mouth

At the Harbour Mouth

HE entrance to Halifax Harbour is blocked by a large irregular island, which leaves to the westward a mile wide passage between itself and the mainland. The shallow, twisting eastern passage is used only by small fishing craft, but this western passage is the water gate of the old city, through which the great ships come and go. The mainland is one granite cliff, steep and high. Its summit is crowned by an old-fashioned round fort with battlements, called York Redoubt, which has been an imperial signal station for more than a century. Modern engineers have made it a second Gibraltar; but that is by the way. At the heel of the island, to seaward, is a low, windworn dune called Thrum Cap, from which series of shoals run out for half a mile. When the southeast winds blow hard, the great waves trip upon these ledges and wall the harbour mouth with breakers. The fishermen still call the outermost reef the Tribune Shoal, from events which took place there more than a century ago.

On the 23rd of November, 1797, about the hour of nine, two men standing outside the gates of York Redoubt and looking seaward, saw a fine large frigate, under British colours, bowling along with a steady wind straight for the fair-lying entrance. One of the men was Lieutenant Brenton Halliburton of the 7th Fusiliers, the Duke of Kent's own regiment, afterwards Sir Brenton Halliburton, Chief Justice of Nova Scotia, and the other was Sergeant McCormack of the same famous corps. They watched the nearing ship closely, and the sergeant, who knew the shoals as well as any tar on board, saw that she was standing into danger.

'If that ship does not alter her course,' he said, 'she will be aground in a quarter of an hour.'

He was too liberal in his time allowance. Within five minutes, the watchers on the cliff saw the good ship check and stop short, as the granite hand of the reef laid firm hold of her keel. The cloud of canvas, instead of filling gracefully, tore frantically this way and that, and the wind carried the noise of the thunderous flapping to the cliff. The tall masts canted over to leeward, and the waves she rode so proudly a moment b'efore, now leaped over the bulwarks and swept he decks. The frigate was hard aground on the Thrum Cap shoals.

It was an annoying accident; and it need not have happened. The ship in trouble had only lately come into the possession of His Britannic Majesty, George the Third. She had been built in some French dockyard by good republican shipwrights, and launched with a brave revolutionary name, *La Tribune,* to do battle with perfidious Albion. On June 8th, 1796, however, she had fallen a prey to H.M.S. *Unicorn* after a chase of two hundred miles, and now was manned with a British crew. In September, 1797, she had formed part of the guard to convoy the Quebec and Newfoundland fleet from Torbay across the Atlantic. By stress of weather, she had been separated from the merchantmen, and early that morning, far out at sea, the mastheads had descried the Nova Scotia coast.

About eight o'clock on this eventful morning, the commander, Captain Scory Barker, paced the quarter-deck.

'Don't you think, Mr. Club,' he said to his sailing master, 'that it would be advisable to lie to and signal for a pilot?'

Mr. Club did not agree with his superior officer. He knew the harbour; the wind was fair; not long since he had worked a forty-four gun ship in, in the teeth of a gale; it would save time, and so on.

Captain Barker hesitated. He knew what was prudent and what ugly consequences followed on the British captains' errors of judgment. Admirals had been shot on the deck of their own ships and victorious officers court-martialed for the very devices by which they gained their victories. England expected her sailors to be infallible. In the navy there is no forgiveness of sins.

At this moment, Mr. John Galvin, master's mate, a passenger, was taking the air on deck. He overheard the colloquy, and spoke up.

'If Captain Barker would accept of my services, I should be happy to assist Mr. Club in taking the ship in. I have had some experience of Halifax Harbour, sir.'

This was an understatement. Mr. Galvin knew the harbour as well as you know your alphabet. But the one thing the British captain of that day could not brook was the faintest sign of interference.

'When your services are required, Mr. Galvin, it will be time enough to volunteer them. I consider Mr. Club quite competent to take the ship in.'

Mr. Galvin's sallow, fever-shrivelled face went red. He had just been exchanged from a sickening French prison in Guadeloupe, where he had been chained leg and leg with his devoted friend, First Lieutenant Thomas Fennell. His health was not good: he drew himself up, bowed in silence, and went below to his cot.

Captain Barker also went below. He had papers to arrange before handing them over to the Port Admiral. There was much to be done before the *Tribune* should be snug at anchor off the dockyard. The sailing master, Mr. James Club, was left in charge of the deck, as well as several other things, such as Captain Barker's reputation and the lives of a whole ship's company. In spite of his assurances, Mr. Club was not perfectly certain of himself; but he knew that if luck favoured him he would get an allowance for pilotage in addition to his pay. So he put a leadsman in the bow-chains, and in the head he stationed a negro sailor, John Casey, upon whose knowledge of the port he relied, to con the ship.

All went well for an hour. Then as the swift frigate rushed on, the leadsman announced rapidly shoaling water. The black man's directions became uncertain.

'Desire Mr. Galvin to come on deck immediately,' cried Club.

'We're standing into shoal water,' he shouted to the black. 'Which way now, Casey?'

'Foh God, Massa Club, Ah don't know.'

At this moment Galvin reached the deck. From the bows came the hoarse cry of the leadsman, 'By the mark, five!'

The master, thoroughly alarmed, rushed to the wheel and took the spokes out of the steersman's hands, as if to wear ship.

'How shall I put my helm, Mr. Galvin?'

Galvin leaped on a carronade to get a sight of the ship's whereabouts; but his aid had been invoked too late. At that moment, the frigate struck and heeled over, and in place of the beautiful order of a ship under sail was unutterable confusion.

Captain Barker was on deck in an instant.

'A — — nice job you've made of it, Mr. Club. You've lost the ship. And do you mean to say, sir,' he added, catching sight of Galvin, 'that you would stand by and see the master run the ship aground after all your officious palaver this morning?'

To such a just and seasonable question there was no possible reply, and Captain Barker was already shouting a dozen orders—to furl the sails—to sound the pumps —to make signals of distress. The crew swarmed on deck and up the yards. In a few minutes the canvas was all taken in, the carpenter reported very little water in the hold; the minute guns were booming, and from the ships in port seven miles away other guns answered.

It was an annoying accident; annoying, nothing more. The wind was rising, to be sure, and everything promised a storm. The situation of the ship was exposed, and might become dangerous; but help was close at hand, and would surely come from

the Dock Yard, to which the wagging telegraph on York Redoubt soon told the news.
The tide was coming in, when the *Tribune*
struck, and if lightened she would float off
at the top of the flood. Still Captain Barker was not happy. A few months before
he had sat on a court-martial which had
dismissed a brother officer from the service
for abandoning his ship, which had gone
ashore, although he had saved the lives of
his crew. England had a great war on her
hands and could not spare a single ship.
It was no comfort that the accident was
not his fault and might have been avoided.
He lost his head.

The tide was high that day at a quarter
to twelve, and if the frigate was to get clear
something must be done at once. Accordingly, one by one, the eighteen heavy
guns on the starboard side were hoisted
out at the yardarms, and one by one they
splashed into the shoal water in her lee.
Then down the slanting deck, the guns of
the port broadside were lowered and
dropped into the sea, except one, which
was kept for signals; and all that afternoon
the deep, heavy, melancholy sound of the
signal gun firing at short intervals min-

gled with the noises of rising wind and dashing water. The manoeuvre was useless; the *Tribune* remained fast on the shoal, heeled over on her starboard side. Indeed, the manoeuvre was worse than useless; it was fatal, as the event proved; for, in the confusion, all the cannons were jettisoned in the lee of the ship, forming there a reef of tumbled iron on the granite, against which the *Tribune* was to break her bones.

The wind was rising to a gale from the southeast and the swelling seas battered the motionless ship with ever-increasing violence, breaking clean over her exposed quarter.

At last the long unexpected help arrived. One heavy barge, after a hard pull of seven miles, reached the stranded ship. Other boats had started, but were forced to put back. But what was the rage and dismay of Captain Barker, when he found that no one above the rank of a boatswain, one Rackum by name, had been sent to his aid. Admiral Murray had b'een recently superseded in the command of the station; and he could, or would, issue no orders. There was no one to share with Captain

Barker the responsibility of abandoning his ship. He flew into a rage with Rackum and would not speak peaceably to him. He even refused to allow the rescue party to quit the ship, much less one man of the crew. One of the army officers who had put off from one of the shore forts to render assistance pointed out that the gale was growing worse and worse, that it would not be high water until after dark, and that in the *Tribune's* exposed position there was great danger of her going to pieces. He begged Captain Barker to land his crew, or at least the women and children.

'Ah, sir!' was the reply, 'I wish your coat was blue instead of red. No! Not a soul quits this ship as long as two planks hold together.'

So the edict went forth! Was he not a British captain, unquestioned despot on his own ship, where his word was law? There was no panic; discipline prevailed. The day wore on; nothing further could be done but wait, wait, wait the tedious tide. Seven miles away the good people of Halifax went about their business, ate their dinners, and took their ease; the Admiral was attending a christening party, says tradition, while at the harbour mouth the tragedy of this doomed ship's company was played to its close.

At six o'clock the tide turned, and as it rose the *Tribune* began to roll to and fro on the shoal. The gloomy day ended in a stormy November night. Then another misfortune befell, for it seems as if relentless fate plucked away hope after hope from these ill-starred men, as a boy pulls an insect to pieces, a limb at a time. The vessel's stern was to the open sea and exposed through long hours to the fullest action of the waves. All afternoon moving hills of water leaped over the quarter and beat against the useless rudder. No bolts or chains could stand such a strain for ever. At last the fastenings parted and the waves wrenched the rudder from its place. With it went the last chance of saving the ship. Even then the crew might have been saved; but the needful order was not given. The rising tide and the waves together half lifted her and she lurched continually from side to side. The masts sloped over, the blocks rattled, the yards clamoured in their slings, and the wind screeched through the cordage. For upward of two hours, the unfortunate ship beat upon her own guns and stove in the planking on her starboard side.

About nine o'clock, driven by the gale, the *Tribune* slid off the shoal into deep water, afloat at last, but without a rudder and with seven feet of water in her hold. So she drifted in the dark before the southeast gale across two miles of raging water to Herring Cove.

Still every effort is made to save the ship. Her chain-pumps are clanking away as fast as sturdy arms can work them, but still the leak gains. Every moment the swaling hulk sinks lower and every moment brings her nearer the deadly lee shore. It is no time to stand on one's dignity. Captain Barker takes counsel with the despised boatswain as one who knows the harbour, and Rackum advises him to let go the bower anchor. It fails to grip the bottom and the battered frigate drifts nearer the granite cliffs, against which the waves are breaking twenty feet high. The doomed men try another desperate shift to save their lives. While the pumps clank on, some seamen cut the cable and others set the jib and foretopmast staysail. If they could but manage with her head canvas to nose inside the harbour mouth less than a mile away, they would be safe. But it is not easy to sail a water-logged ship without a helm in a November storm. No expedient will bring up the drifting ship. When they are almost under the cliff, as a last desperate resource they drop the second anchor, in thirteen fathoms of water. For a wonder it holds. To lighten her, the mizzen-mast is cut away; the *Tribune* rides a trifle easier, and there seems to be a faint hope that she may outlive the storm.

It is a vain hope; the *Tribune* is at her last moorings. After all her cruises, she has come to lay her bones at the foot of this wild Nova Scotian cliff. Now there is no escape for her. In sixty minutes after she floated at Thrum Cap, she crossed that two-mile stretch of water and brought up just three ship's lengths south of Herring Cove, a narrow, curving fissure in the iron coast. To-day the banks are lined by a quaint fishing village, which then consisted of only a few scattered huts. The drifting *Tribune* just missed the entrance, and safety. About half-past nine, she was observed to lurch violently twice and then go down all standing, as a ship does when she is evenly full of water. She carried down with her, not only her own crew, but some sailors' wives and children, and men sent from the Dock Yard to the ship's assistance. Some sank at once; and some were battered against the cliff. But the fore and main masts remained well above water, and nearly one hundred survivors managed to get into the rigging.

It was only a temporary respite from death. Again there was a choosing by fate. One by one the exhausted men lost their hold and were swept off into the sea. About midnight, the mainmast gave way, and only ten regained the rigging. When morning broke there were only eight alive and all but two were so near dead with exhaustion as to be indifferent whether they were rescued or not. People on shore came down to the point opposite to where the ship sank and kept fires blazing all night. They were close enough to talk with those clinging to the wreck; but no effort was made at rescue.

Day came; the weary hours dragged on and still no attempt was made to save the perishing sailors. The Herring Cove men are not proud of their forbears' conduct; they would not do so to-day. The fact remains that nothing was done until about eleven o'clock on the morning of the 24th.

Then a boy, a mere child of thirteen, put off single-handed in his skiff. He had to row down the cove, then out into a perfect witch's cauldron of breaking waves, recoil, eddy, and countercurrent. Every moment he was in deadly peril; every moment he was straining every muscle to the utmost. How he managed remains something of a miracle; but the fact is undoubted that he not only made head against that tremendous sea, but brought his skiff round and backed it in as near to the foretop as he dared. How eagerly his approach must have been watched by those eight drenched, numb, despairing men and with what alternations of hope and fear! The only two who can bear a hand are Dunlop and Monroe, and now they have a chance for life, surely they will take it. But that was not the mettle of the British tar in those great and gallant days. The two heroes on the wreck give up their last chance of life, and with infinite pains and difficulty fasten a rope round an insensible comrade, who only mutters a wish to be left to die in peace, and, as the boy brings his frail skiff alongside, they lower him into the little dancing ark of safety. This man is no other than John Galvin, master's mate, who bears a charmed life. When the *Tribune* sank he was below, directing the men at the chain-pumps. Washed up the hatchway into the waist, he was swept overboard, and sank, striking a rock. As he rose, three drowning men grappled him. He dived and they loosed their hold. He rose to the surface, clambered into the maintop and seated himself on an arm-chest secured there. About midnight, the mainmast fell and only ten of the forty clinging to it regained their hold. Now while he lies like a log in the bottom of the boat, a second man is lowered into it by the two great-hearted sailormen, and perilously overloaded the 'flat' starts for the cove. There is no risk to be run in returning, and wind and wave help instead of hindering the little boat. The men on the wreck strain their dull eyes after her until she disappears into the cove and safety. A long interval elapses. How long it must have seemed to the poor fellows clinging to their frail support above the waves! and how slight must have seemed the hope of rescue by a mere boy! At last the little boat with the single youthful oarsman in it appears once more at the opening of the cliff and slowly—very slowly, comes towards them. But the boy has overtaxed his strength. His hands are cramped on his paddles, the muscles of his arms and back are strained to starting; in spite of his breathless labour, he shivers in his soaking jersey, and pull gallantly as he will, he can make no headway. The waves sweep him back; he grows weaker and weaker, and, at last, to save his life, he is forced to put about. But his defeat accomplished more than his success. The men were shamed into action by his glorious example of courage and determination. A volunteer crew was soon found for the jolly-boat, in which four men had escaped the night before. Within another hour, the last survivor was safely landed. Only twelve men were left of a fine ship's company of nearly 250: among them, it is pleasant to find, were the two heroic sailors, Dunlop and Monroe.

11

That is the story of the *Tribune*. All
this tragedy was played to its close at the
harbour mouth between Thrum Cap and
Herring Cove Head. The shoal where she
struck is called the Tribune Shoal to this
day. Any fisherman or pilot will point it
out to the curious, and, by laying the accent on the second syllable, prove the
French origin of the word. As for the
hero itself, little has been handed down.
The rescued sailors could not say enough
about his courage and his kindness. The
great people of Halifax took him up, petted
him, and showed their appreciation of his
heroism by trying to make a gentleman of
him. The Duke of Kent praised him publicly and got him a midshipman's berth
on the flagship. But he pined under the
restrictions of naval discipline and was allowed to return to his old way of life. Apparently he was a fisherman's apprentice,
without kith or kin in Herring Cove. There
is a tradition that he was weak in the head,
which is not borne out by the skill and determination shown in the rescue. He
must have been a simple soul. When asked
by the Royal Duke in his princely way to
name his own reward for his golden deed,

he requested—says tradition—a pair of corduroy breeches! His name is not certainly known. Tradition says it was 'Joe Cracker,' otherwise, Joseph Shortt. The Herring Cove fishermen remember his nickname, and say that he went away to sea and was never heard of again. They believe that there is an accumulation of pension awaiting his heirs in England. They know well where the wreck lies, for their nets foul on the jagged timbers every now and then. The *Tribune's* dead are all buried in one field near where they perished. But for the dauntless fisher boy, like Browning's hero,

Name and deed alike are lost,
Not a pillar or a post
  In his Croisic keeps alive the feat as it befell.

VII

Godfrey of the *Rover*

Godfrey of the 'Rover'

E are rather ashamed of it nowadays and offer various excuses for the behaviour of our grandfathers, but, in the good old times, privateering was a recognised and lawful branch of commercial speculation. To fit out private vessels of war to prey on the enemy's commerce seemed to our ancestors a laudable act of patriotism. They annoyed the King's enemies, and put money in their own purses, and their robust consciences never felt a qualm.

In three great wars Nova Scotia had stood staunchly by the mother country and aided her, while defending herself, by this very practice of privateering. Scarcely had the Seven Years' War broken out before Halifax merchants were busy arming, victualling, manning all kinds of craft against the enemies of George II. All through the American Revolution and the

long wars with the French republic and
Napoleon, right down to Waterloo, Nova
Scotia privateers scoured the seas. Not
only the capital but almost every port—
Yarmouth, Liverpool, Annapolis Royal—
fitted out private vessels of war. Their
doings made a fascinating chapter of provincial history which remains to be written.

The first step was for solid business men
of old Halifax, like Malachy Salter and
Robert Saunderson, to obtain a letter
of marque from the governor. This was
a commission empowering a ship not in
the regular navy to make war for the benefit of her owners. There were some necessary restrictions. They had to give substantial bonds to fulfil the conditions on
which the commission was granted, such as
sending in all prizes to the Court of Vice-
Admiralty to be adjudged, to keep an accurate log, and to report all information
as to the enemy's movements. This meant
becoming responsible for various sums,
from £1,500 to £3,000. More money was
needed to fit the vessels out. Cannon,
swivels, cohorns, cutlasses, muskets, pistols, boarding-pikes, food, supplies, powder
and shot, 'furniture' were not to be had for

love. Privateers were heavily armed and manned. The little schooner *Lawrence*, the first Halifax privateer, measured only a hundred tons, but she carried fourteen four-pounder carriage guns, twenty swivels, and a complement of a hundred men. The reasons for such a heavy armament and such a large crew are plain. A swivel was a very small cannon, sometimes no bigger than a blunderbuss, fitted to light carriages which might be trundled easily about the decks, perched on the bulwarks, or even mounted in the tops. Sometimes they were provided with flare mouths, to make the charge spread. Elizabethan sailors called them 'murdering-pieces.' They were intended to repel boarders or cover the rush of their attack, and they corresponded to machine-guns of the present day. All these things point to a consistent policy of close action. When the privateer fought, she fought yardarm to yardarm.

The crew were caught by bait like this:

Seamen and able-bodied landsmen who wish to acquire riches and honour are invited to repair on board the *Revenge*, private ship of war, now lying in Halifax Harbour, mounting thirty carriage guns, with cohorns, swivels, etc., bound for a cruise to the southward for four months vs. the French and all H.M. enemies, and then return to the harbour.

In war time the old Halifax newspapers were filled with such advertisements. A few months later they would contain notifications that all who were actually on board the *Revenge* at the capture of such and such vessels would receive their prize money from the ship's agent at a given time and place. Apparently there was no lack of 'seamen and able-bodied landsmen' ready to jump at the 'riches and honour' without a thought for the bullet or splinter that might lay them low, long before the ship returned to Halifax Harbour. There was the risk of drowning, of capture, of short shrift at the hands of hostile regular combatants, and of the terrors of a foreign prison; but our grandfathers faced them all. Governor Lawrence complained that all the labouring men in Halifax had gone off in privateers.

It is easy to understand why privateering even in its palmy days was looked down upon. It was a form of mercantile speculation, and the speculators must have their dividends. Primarily the privateer was not a battleship but a commerce-destroyer. She ran down vessels that could not fight, and ran from those that could. Grim stories linger round our seaports of lawless plunder, of boats armed and sent ashore at night to raid defenceless farms, of fingers cut from dead men's hands for the sake of the rings, of shiploads of gold and silver plate taken from desecrated churches. 'You'll observe there were many things happened we don't care to talk about,' is the saying of one old privateersman, which has been handed down. When it comes to putting the thumbscrews on a merchant captain and making him dance round his own deck to the strains of a foc's'l fiddle, you may know how far an old-fashioned 'sea-solicitor' would go for the sake of loot. To overhaul a solitary fisherman in his sloop and rob him of a couple of barrels of salt and a bolt of Russia duck was no uncommon exploit. Almost every Nova Scotia coast town has its own story of foreign privateers landing and plundering. American privateers laid a mortgage on Lunenburg which has never been paid or foreclosed. The plain truth is that privateering was licensed piracy.

Some ventures were extremely successful. The *Retaliation* brought in fourteen prizes in one year; the *Sir John Sherbrooke* captured sixteen in a single cruise, while the *Liverpool Packet,* a fierce little wasp of sixty-seven tons, with a crew of forty-five men, made nineteen captures in two cruises. In one year, 1813, our Nova Scotian privateers made prize of 106 vessels. Such luck meant 'riches,' if not 'honour,' for the owners and the ship's company. No wonder privateering flourished. It gave speedier and richer returns than western real estate.

At the same time, when necessary, these licensed pirates were perfectly ready to fight. The ships were speedy sailers, well handled, bristling with arms and swarming with men, and they must have been formidable at close quarters. On her return voyage from Bermuda in 1757, the little *Lawrence* did her best to engage a French sloop-of-war, but the Frenchman ran for it. On Monday, July 10, 1780, the Nova Scotian privateer brig *Resolution,* commanded by Captain Thomas Ross, fought a fierce action with the 'rebel' ship *Viper* off Sambro Light. True to her name, the

Resolution struck her flag only when she had lost eighteen of her crew, killed and wounded, while thirty-three were down on the *Viper's* deck, and both vessels were badly mauled. There must have been hundreds of such fights all up and down the seas, duly logged and now forgotten.

The most brilliant of all privateer actions in which Nova Scotians took part is the fight of the brig *Rover* with a Spanish schooner and three gunboats off Cape Blanco on the 10th of September, 1800. The record has been preserved in the very words of an eyewitness, her captain, the man who directed the fight to a successful issue. Both he and his battle are well-nigh forgotten now, but there are many reasons why they should not be allowed to slip into oblivion. Wherefore I tell the tale once more; it has not been told for half a century.

The *Rover* was a little brig of a hundred tons, built in the year 1800 at the pleasant, picturesque seaport of Liverpool, Nova Scotia. *The Naval Chronicle* states that in the four years previous twelve or fifteen ships of war had been fitted out in Nova Scotia, and half of them had come from this one tiny village. That was the way in the old days. The same men cut down the timber in the forest, hauled it to the shipyard, built the ship, manned the ship, and, on occasion, fought the ship. The *Rover* carried fourteen four-pounders, a favourite weapon with old-time privateers, and a complement of fifty-five boys, men, and officers. Most were local fishermen. According to trustworthy tradition handed down in the Morton family of Liverpool, the *Rover* carried in addition a large gun amidships which was loaded with chain. The captain of this gun was an old experienced sailor. On the 22nd of May she received her letter of marque, under the authority of the Lieutenant-Governor, Sir John Wentworth, Bart., and, on the 4th of June, the King's Birthday, she sailed from her native port 'on a cruise against the enemies of Great Britain.' Her captain was Alexander Godfrey, who is described as a big man, 'of an exceedingly quiet demeanour, and modest and retiring disposition.' Big, quiet, plain, two-handed men of the same blood and name are still to be found in Queen's County. Godfrey was evidently a finished sailor and a bonny fighter. His account of his great battle is in perfect accord with the account of his character. It is simple, modest, manly. He handled his pen almost as well as he handled his brig.

The *Rover's* first exploit shows her spirit. On her thirteenth day out, sailing the open, desolate seas, well to the east of the West Indies and almost on the Tropic of Cancer (23° N. and 54° W., to be precise), she sighted a cluster of sail. The cluster resolved itself into a full-rigged ship, a schooner, and four brigs. The schooner showed sixteen guns; so did one brig, while another showed six. They 'drew up together, apparently with an intention of engaging us.' The odds were six to one, and the chances were all in the enemy's favour. What happened next throws light on the *Rover's* discipline and the relations which existed between Godfrey and his crew. He was no arbitrary tyrant, but the first among his equals. He consulted with his ship's company whether or not to attack this squadron single-handed. The privateersmen were full of fight. Like Moloch's, their counsel was for open war, and the *Rover,* with her red

ensign flying, bore down on six vessels,
two of which were more heavily armed
than herself. 'But so soon as the enemy
perceived our intentions, they, by signal
from the schooner, dispersed, each taking
a different course before we got within
gunshot of them.' In two instances, flight
was vain. The speedy *Rover,* 'after a
few hours chase,' ran down the ship, evidently a lumbering whaler laden with
sperm oil from the South Seas, and one of
the brigs with a cargo of wine from
Madeira. Both were American vessels
which had been captured by the schooner,
a French privateer, only a short time before. Under cover of night she got away
with her three remaining prizes. As she
carried sixteen guns, all heavier than those
of the *Rover,* and a crew of 155 men, her
failure to abide the Nova Scotian's onset
is hard to understand.

What happened between the 17th of
June and the 10th of September is not told
us, but in the interval the *Rover* had succeeded in getting herself excessively dis-
liked by the enemies of King George III
all along the Spanish Main, for a special
expedition was fitted out to effect her

capture. It consisted of a schooner, the *Santa Ritta,* armed with ten six-pounders and two twelve-pounder carronades, and three gunboats of unknown tonnage, armament, and crews. The schooner carried 125 men, and the gunboats probably half as many. The Spaniards of Costa Rica were going to make sure of the obnoxious stranger.

The 10th of September was an eventful day for the 'Rovers.' As they were cruising near Cape Blanco, they sighted a Spanish schooner, which 'we chased on shore and destroyed,' reports Godfrey with Spartan brevity. Immediately after, the wind fell, and while they lay becalmed, they spied the *Santa Ritta* and her three consorts making for them under the red and yellow flag of Spain. The *Santa Ritta* had her flag nailed to the mast. This was to be a battle *à outrance*. If the captain did not bring back Godfrey's head, he was to lose his own, says tradition. On the other hand, Godfrey realised the desperate nature of the approaching battle, and placed his cabin-boy in the magazine with a slow match burning in his hand, under strict orders to blow up the ship, if the Spaniards boarded and won the deck. Then the fickle breeze shifted and enabled the *Rover* to draw out from the land, while her enemies manned their sweeps—the long heavy oars run through the vessel's side—and gained on her fast. They advanced, firing from their bow guns. At least three of them did, but the third gunboat, not liking the look of affairs, held off and remained throughout an idle spectator of the fray. To meet their attack, the *Rover* also manned her sweeps and maintained a fire from 'two guns pointed from the stern.' What happened next is best told in Godfrey's own simple, manly words.

'As the enemy drew near we engaged them with muskets and pistols, keeping with oars the stern of the *Rover* toward them, and having our guns well loaded with great and small shot, ready against we should come to close quarters. When we heard the commander of the schooner give orders to the two gunboats to board us, one on the larboard bow and the other on the larboard waist, I suffered them to advance in that position until they came within about fifteen yards, still firing on them with small arms and stern guns. I then manned the oars on the larboard side and pulled the *Rover* round so as to bring her starboard broadside to bear athwart the schooner's bow, and poured into her a whole broadside of great and small shot, which raked her deck fore and aft while it was full of men ready for boarding. I instantly shifted over to the other side and raked both gunboats in the same manner, which must have killed and wounded a great number of those on board of them, and done great damage to their boats.'

This was not a trained and seasoned fighter, apprenticed to war and experienced in sea battles, but a Province trader who had just taken up the profession of arms. He is attacked on two sides at once by vastly superior numbers, and on the spur. of necessity invents a brilliant manoeuvre which leaves the advantage in his hands. He coolly allows the two gunboats to approach within a biscuit-toss of him. Then, by means of his sweeps, he spins his vessel round, away from them and at right angles to his other and more dangerous enemy, the schooner, and while in that position fires his six guns, crammed to the muzzle with deadly missiles, into her crowded deck. Instantly he repeats the manoeuvre on the two gunboats, which must now have been close alongside. The sailors drop the sweeps on the port side, rush to the starboard side and, by main strength, spin the *Rover* round till her larboard battery is brought to bear. These two broadsides thwarted the Spanish commander's well-laid plan of attack.

Godfrey continues: 'I then commenced a close action with the schooner, which lasted three glasses, and having disabled her sails and rigging much, and finding her fire grow slack, I took advantage of a slight air of wind to back my head sails, which brought my stern on board of the schooner, by which we were enabled to board her, at which time the gunboats shoved off, apparently in a shattered condition.'

'Close action' still meant a long and doubtful fight with a superior force. It lasted for an hour and a half, the time on board ship then being measured, as everyone knows, by sand in a glass, which took thirty minutes to run out. Through all the confusion of the fight some one must have watched that glass and turned it over as the last grains fell. While big guns and little guns, muskets and pistols, barked and snapped, in a hanging cloud of smoke the vigilant captain of the *Rover* watched for an opportunity to deal his enemy a decisive blow. At last he noticed a slight breeze and skilfully trimmed his canvas so that the *Rover* drifted backward till she ground the side of the *Santa Ritta*. As the vessels touched, Godfrey sprang to the Spaniard's deck at the head of the boarding party.

They found a shambles. On the bloody deck fourteen men lay dead and seventeen wounded. The scuppers were running blood. No one could deny that the Spaniards had fought with desperate resolution. Deprived of their officers, the survivors of the crew fled from the deck, while the Spanish flag still floated at the mast-head as from an unconquered ship.

Then followed a picturesque incident. A young Spanish lad ran up from below and swarmed into the main-rigging to the truck. With his knife, he slashed away the Spanish flag, which drooped and fell into the sea. If it could only have been preserved as a trophy! Swiftly the sailor lad returned to the deck and, falling on his knees before Godfrey, begged for mercy.

Godfrey put his hand on the boy's head and assured him that he would not be harmed; but he took the precaution of drawing the youngster's knife from its sheath and throwing it into the sea. Tradition continues that Godfrey adopted the young Spaniard and gave him an English education. Every officer but one who was in charge of a small detachment of soldiers had been killed.

The unhurt Spanish prisoners outnumbered the victorious 'Rovers' nearly two to one. Godfrey could not guard them, so four days later he landed all but eight, 'taking an obligation from them not to serve against his Majesty until regularly exchanged.' Like every good captain, he gives the credit to his men. 'My ship's company, including officers and boys, was only forty-five in number, and behaved with that courage and spirit which British seamen always show when fighting the enemies of their country. It is with infinite pleasure that I add that I had not a man hurt.' And they had accounted for at least fifty-four Spaniards!

Never had a privateer a luckier maiden cruise. In addition to his other captures,

Godfrey took a sloop and a Spanish schooner, and all his prizes were safely navigated back to Nova Scotia. They must have paid for the *Rover* twice over. Honour was the share of the privateersmen as well as riches, for they had fought at long odds and won. Best of all, when the *Rover* dropped anchor in Liverpool Harbour on October 17, 1800, not a single member of the crew was missing. Before that day passed, Godfrey penned the dispatch which, printed in the *Naval Chronicle* for February 1801, forms the basis of my narrative. Britain wanted such fighting men and offered Godfrey a commission in the royal navy, but he declined the honour. When a lull came in 1802 in the long war with France, Godfrey disarmed his privateer and returned to his peaceful trading in fish and lumber with the West Indies. In 1803 he died of yellow fever and was buried near Kingston, Jamaica, in an unknown, unmarked grave. He should have a statue in the Liverpool market-place.

Half a century ago, a local bard was moved to celebrate the hero in this strain:

A niche for a name in thy temple of fame,
  Oh, Acadie, gem of the occident wave,

The Muse and the Poet beseechingly claim
For Godfrey, thy Godfrey, the good and the
brave.

He certainly deserves his niche, but
hitherto the desires of the muse and the
poet have been frustrate of their hope.

The Glory of the *Shannon*

The Glory of the 'Shannon'

OR those faint hearts who fear that Britain is doomed to speedy decline, no better tonic could be prescribed than reading the naval history of the Great War. From 1792 to 1815, Britain was fighting for bare life; she saved herself and she saved Europe by her unconquerable fleet. Everyone knows Nelson's name and the fame of Trafalgar and the Nile; but, in those great and gallant days, there were a thousand little battles which have passed into oblivion.

For more than twenty years, British ships of war of all ratings were fighting almost daily in every sea. From the Poles to the Tropics, by day and night, at all seasons, in fair weather and storm, they were chasing their foes, or circling about them in black powder smoke, or hammering away yard-arm to yard-arm, or firing as they ran, or flinging the bare-foot boarders, stripped

185

to the waist and cutlass in hand, on the hostile decks in final desperate assault. But who knows, or cares, how the *Junon* beat off fifteen gunboats in Hampton Roads, or how the *Unicorn* ran down the *Tribune* in a chase of two hundred and ten miles, or how the *Amelia* battered the *Arethuse* in the tropic moonlight, with the muzzles of their guns almost touching? Such fighting will never be seen again. It passed with the days of sail; but the tradition is alive in the King's ships—dreadnought, cruiser, torpedo-boat, and submarine—of the present day. The tale may be read at length in the neglected chronicle of James. There is not a page in it but is calculated to foster pride of race and admiration for mere human courage and devotion to duty.

Of all these sea-duels, the most famous and memorable is the brief and terrible encounter between the *Shannon* and the *Chesapeake,* off Boston lighthouse, a hundred years ago. It is remembered and it deserves to be remembered for many reasons. Since Trafalgar, British ships had been regarded as invincible. The war of 1812 began, however, with a series of unexpected reverses at sea. Britain heard with incredulity, rage, and gloom that British captains had lowered their flag to the despised Yankees. The *Guerriere* and the *Java* had struck to the *Constitution,* and the *Macedonian* to the *United States.* Our ancestors felt as we felt when we learned that a British regiment with arms in their hands had surrendered in the field to a ragged Boer commando. Nothing could efface such black shame. Although these single-ship actions had no effect whatever upon the course and upshot of the war, their results depressed the British unduly, and naturally and justly elated the Americans. The British frigates were unlucky beyond doubt; but the Americans deserved to win because they had bigger, better built ships, because they paid more attention to gunnery, because they were bold and skilful seamen, and because they adopted the favourite British tactics of dashing attack and close action, while foreigners preferred the safer game of long bowls. As Lucas pertinently remarks, war is not knight-errantry, but business, and the surest way to defeat your enemy is to attack him in superior force.

Nowhere outside of England was the course of the Great War followed with more eager interest than in the good city of Halifax. In and out of the harbour passed famous ships which had fought under Nelson, and in the garrison had been quartered historic regiments which were to win fresh laurels in the Peninsula or at Waterloo. Officers of the army and navy mingled with Halifax society and married Halifax girls. De Quincey has told how the mail coaches carried the news of victory down from London. 'Oh, those were days of power, gallant days, bustling days, worth the bravest days of chivalry at least.' When the news of a victory reached Halifax, the merchants hired a military band to play patriotic marches and loyal tunes on the roof of the market building, while they drank success to British arms in their reading-room opposite. The whole town would be illuminated and parties of young people would stroll about admiring the effect of windows full of candles. When the *Guerriere* was lost, the whole city was plunged in gloom.

According to local tradition, the famous fight began in Mr. William Minns' bookshop, opposite the Parade. An old Hali-

gonian remembered Captain Broke coming
in with a walking-stick in his hand and his
epaulets setting firmly but carelessly on his
shoulders, and saying, 'Well, Minns, I am
going to Boston.' Boston Bay, between
Cape Ann and Cape Cod, was a favourite
cruising ground, for into that funnel poured
a great tide of American commerce. Broke
further told Mr. Minns that he intended 'to
challenge the *Constitution*.' He had been
a frigate commander for eighteen years and
had never encountered an enemy's vessel of
the same class. Mr. Minns ventured to
think that the *Shannon's* eighteen-
pounders would have no chance with the
Constitution's twenty - four - pounders.
Broke replied that he intended to fight
yard-arm to yard-arm and to depend on the
devotion of his three hundred men, 'each
of whom, will, I know, follow me to the
death, and stand by me to the last.' He
would trust more to boarding than to the
calibre of his guns. If this ancient Hali-
gonian's memory served him aright, Broke
had decided on his tactics before he left
port. The *Shannon* was already famous
for her many captures and for her captain's
foible of giving his share—always the lion's

share—of the prize money to his crew. By such treatment, by firm discipline, and by constant gun-drill, Broke had made his frigate perhaps the most effective fighting machine of her class in the navy.

Why did Broke mention the *Constitution* in his chat with Mr. Minns? He had many reasons for wanting to fight this particular frigate. Every post-captain in the navy was burning to wipe out the disgrace of the British surrenders. 'We must catch one of those great American ships . . . and send her home for a show,' Broke wrote to his wife. But he had, I venture to think, a special reason for naming the *Constitution*. That vessel had defeated and taken two British frigates and Broke had been a member of the court-martial held on young Captain Dacres for losing his ship. The court-martial had been held on board H.M.S. *Africa,* a Trafalgar ship, in Halifax harbour. Only a naval officer can appreciate Broke's feelings. To sit in judgment on a brother in arms, whose sword has been taken from him, to know that your verdict may ruin his career is a severe ordeal. Dacres was freely blamed as a young and inexperienced officer in giving up his ship too soon. A Boston canard stated that he had fought two duels in consequence of his inglorious surrender. The facts are that he was the first to own defeat, and that he was unlucky. He fought his ship until every mast went over the side and the *Guerriere* was wallowing, an unmanageable hulk, in the trough of the sea. It was impossible to work her main-deck guns, the sea swilled through the open ports, and the *Constitution* simply chose her own position where not a gun of the *Guerriere* could reach her and proceeded at her leisure to pound her helpless enemy to splinters. Dacres himself was wounded and seventy-seven out of his crew of three hundred men were struck down before he gave in. It is difficult to see what else he could have done. None the less to lose one's ship for whatever reason is black disgrace. There are no excuses in the navy.

On March 13, 1813, the *Shannon* and her sister ship, the *Tenedos,* weighed anchor, and, two towers of white sail, glided magnificently down the harbour past George's and Thrum Cap to the open sea. They went to cruise in company off Boston Bay, where homing prizes flocked thickest. It

13

was their business and duty to destroy commerce; but what they hoped for was a battle with a couple of the four American frigates refitting in Boston harbour. They were to catch as many of the enemy's merchantmen as they could, make prisoners of their crews, and send the captured vessels with the minimum number of British sailors to navigate them to Halifax, there to be adjudged in the court of vice-admiralty. Prizes meant prize-money, and 'dashing in coaches,' so service in frigates was much more popular than in the great three-deckers, the lumbering sea-wagons, whose business was to fight in a line with the like ships of the foe. Why frigates hunted in couples is obvious. One could support the other with her guns and boats, if engaged near land, and render aid if her consort in chase should get on shore. For more than two months the *Shannon* and *Tenedos* plied their trade, overhauling luckless merchantmen and bringing them to, or beating out to sea with scanty canvas when the cold easterly gales with rain and snow would force them on shore. The *Shannon* took some twenty-five prizes, which were destroyed because Broke would not weaken his crew by sending men off in them. The only exceptions he made were vessels belonging to Halifax, re-captures and the property of British subjects, but he begrudged a single one of his three hundred, who 'would follow him anywhere.' He needed them all to work the ship and fight the guns.

On the first of May, the *President* and the *Congress* eluded the vigilance of the British cruisers and, favoured by the fog, sailed out to sea. Of the two that remained in harbour refitting, the *Chesapeake* was nearly ready for a cruise by the end of the month. Broke took a course which recalls the palmy days of chivalry. He sent Captain Lawrence of the *Chesapeake* a formal challenge to come out and fight him ship to ship. It was as courteous as an invitation to dinner or to spend a month at Brokehall. He gives the number of his crew and of his guns. He mentions that he is short of provisions and water. He has detached the *Tenedos,* so no British ship will interfere with the duello.

This amazing letter begins: 'Sir,—As the *Chesapeake* appears now ready for sea, I request you will do me the favour to meet the *Shannon* with her and try the fortune of our respective flags.' It ends, 'Choose your terms—but let us meet.'

This was not the only instance of a British captain trying to obtain 'the satisfaction of a gentleman,' in those days when a case of hair-triggers found a place in their portmanteaus as naturally as their razors. Sir John Yeo, of the *Southampton,* challenged Porter, of the *Essex,* and Parker, of the 'bold *Menelaus,*' sent a message to Mallet, of the *Atalante,* of the same tenor as Broke's. There seems to be some doubt whether or not Lawrence received the letter. At all events, he acted as if he had.

In the captain of the *Chesapeake,* Broke had a foeman worthy of his steel. Physically he was a giant, as a fighting captain he was bold and successful. Only a short time previously, in the *Hornet,* he had defeated the *Peacock* by the same methods that had proved so effective in other single ship actions, dashing attack, good seamanship, and first-class gunnery. His word to his crew just before the fight began was '*Peacock* her.' His ship was as fit as the ship-wrights and riggers could make her. He had a picked crew. No vessel ever went into a fight with better chances of success. On this beautiful June day she began to spread her canvas at noon and, as light airs prevailed, set all her sails, even her stunsails, and proceeded slowly down the bay, a stately white cloud, with three large American flags ruffling from her rigging and a broad banner at the fore inscribed, 'Sailors' Rights and Free Trade.'

Under shortened sail the *Shannon* tacked to and fro, waiting for her adversary to close. Only one British flag flew at her mizzen. 'Mayn't we have three ensigns, sir, like she has?' a sailor asked. 'No,' said Broke, 'we have always been an unassuming ship.' A number of pleasure-boats followed the *Chesapeake* down the harbour to see the fight, and a dinner was prepared in Boston to celebrate the victory.

In those days of sail, there were two well recognised kinds of tactics. One was to open fire at extreme range, keep away, and aim at the rigging of the hostile ship in the hope of knocking away a spar and so render her unmanageable. The other was desperate 'in-fighting,' laying your ship as close as possible to the foe, grappling with him, and turning the sea-fight into a land fight

by invading his decks with a rush of boarders. This was the favourite British method
and the battle of the *Shannon* and the
Chesapeake is a classic example of it.

It took all afternoon for the *Chesapeake*
to reach the *Shannon*. At ten minutes to
six the fight began, and all was over by five
minutes past. This most famous fight
lasted just a quarter of an hour.

You are to imagine the two fine frigates
drifting slowly nearer and nearer in the
lovely June weather, both heading east and
sailing on parallel lines. On both, every
gun is loaded and run out; around each gun
is grouped each gun crew, all along the low,
dim perspective of the main-deck; the
powder-monkeys are ready to carry cartridge from the magazine; cutlasses and
boarding-pikes are laid out for the boarders;
down in the cock-pit, the surgeon and his
mates are waiting with lint and bandages,
saws and knives for the first wounded man
who will be carried down to them. Naval
gunnery was not a fine art in the old days.
The *Shannon's* main-deck guns were
loaded alternately with two round-shot or
with one round-shot and one grape, all
along her broadside. Imagine, if you can,

the effect of these missiles fired into a wooden ship, at pistol-shot range, when you could see the faces of the men you fired at.

Broke had made his little speech before action to the 'Shannons' from the quarter-deck. They were 'to kill the men.' 'Go quietly to your quarters and don't cheer,' he ended. The *Chesapeake* was now close; her crew gave three cheers; but it was 'still' all over the British ship. As the bow of the overtaking *Chesapeake* reached slowly past the stern of the *Shannon* the captain of the fourteenth gun pulled his lanyard, the gun roared and the shot was observed to strike near the enemy's second port. Then a bow-gun spoke; then the rest as fast as they could be fired, but there were only two broadsides fired. Now Broke's gun-drill told, and the effect of the well served guns at close range was deadly. The two frigates were shrouded in smoke. Slowly the head of the *Chesapeake* turned away and her stern ground along the *Shannon's* side towards the bow until she was checked by the fluke of the *Shannon's* anchor catching in the *Chesapeake's* quarter port. In this position she was raked by the British guns.

This was another critical moment of the fight. The *Shannon's* boatswain William Stevens had fought under Rodney in the Battle of the Saints and was now nearly sixty years of age. As the ships scraped, he went over the side and began to lash them together. He had his left arm hacked off by repeated sword-cuts and he was mortally wounded by musketry, but his lashings held long enough to make a bridge for the boarders. Broke, who had run forward, saw the Americans flinching from the quarter-deck guns, and calling, 'Follow me who can!' stepped from the *Shannon's* gangway rail to the *Chesapeake's* aftermost carronade and so to her deck, with about twenty men from the forecastle. He had ordered the main-deck boarders and quarter-deck men to be called away, but he did not wait for them. Not a man or an officer was to be seen and the British swept forward over the bloody deck. At the gangways, there was some slight resistance, but the Americans were driven below, or they flung down their arms. Never was a speedier triumph.

Two unlucky incidents took place almost at the same instant, at the opposite ends of

the captured ship. The boarders had swept
the deck clear of the foe in a few breathless
minutes, and reached the forecastle. Here
the Americans threw down their weapons.
Broke placed a sentry over them and turned
to give orders to fire into the *Chesapeake's*
main-top, when three of the Americans who
had surrendered snatched weapons from the
deck and rushed at him. The sentry's shout
warned him of his danger. He wheeled
about, parried the midmost man's pike
thrust and wounded him in the face, but one
of his comrades stunned Broke with the
butt-end of a musket and the other laid his
head open with a cutlass. His assailants
were at once cut down by the furious 'Shannons,' but the wounded captain was never
the same man again.

As the first lieutenant Watt followed
Broke over the side with the quarter-deck
boarders, he was shot in the foot and fell on
his knee. Quickly rising he gave orders to
fire one of the *Shannon's* six-pounders into
the mizzen-top, whence he had received his
wound. According to Dr. Akins, a sailor
had run on b'oard with a small British flag
on a boat-hook. With his own hand, Watt
lowered the Stars-and-Stripes from the miz-

zen-peak and bent on the British flag. In the tangle of colours and halliards, he bent on the British flag below, instead of above, the American, and when he began to haul the two up, the American was uppermost. To the men of the *Shannon* peering through the thick smoke, this could have only one meaning, and they fired at the dim figures on the quarter-deck with deadly aim. A grape-shot carried away the top of Watt's head and killed four or five of the men with him. Then the flags were hoisted properly. The Americans below surrendered and the fight was done.

Two broadsides and a swift rush of boarders and the battle was over. Before the following yachts could realise what had happened, the American crew were in the very handcuffs they had laid out on the deck for the British, and the two frigates were making sail for Halifax. This was the most murderous fight in the long annals of single-ship actions. The victorious *Shannon* lost eighty-three killed and wounded and the *Chesapeake* one hundred and forty-six. Almost one man out of every three engaged was struck down.

Sunday, June 6, 1813, was a very beautiful

day in Halifax, a day long remembered. During the morning service, some one came into St. Paul's, whispered to a friend in the garrison pew and hastily left the church. An observer thought of fire and followed him. Soon the church was empty. All the city was on the wharves and house-tops cheering like mad a procession of two frigates coming slowly up the harbour past George's Island. The first was a 'little dirty black ship,' said Aunt Susan Etter, who saw them with her own eyes as a girl of thirteen, 'and the other was a big fine ship.' The first was the *Shannon,* her paint sadly weathered by three months cruising, and the second was her prize the *Chesapeake,* still fresh and glittering from the Boston shipyard. As they passed, the spectators observed that the decks were being swabbed and that the scuppers were running red. The bands played and the ships in harbour manned their yards in honour of the victory. The two vessels anchored near the Dock Yard and at once began to send the wounded ashore.

No visitors were allowed on board the *Shannon,* for the captain's head wounds made quiet imperative; but two eye-witnesses have left on record what they saw 'tween decks of the *Chesapeake*. Both were boys. One writes:

She was like a perfect charnel house. Her main deck from forward of the mast to the extreme stern of the vessel was covered with hammocks, in which lay the wounded, the dying, and the dead, each hammock having a cord or rope suspended to it from the roof of the deck, so that the poor fellows might lay hold of it and ease themselves up .... Very many ... lay writhing in their wounds.

The other boy was Thomas Chandler Haliburton, the creator of 'Sam Slick.' He gives more details:

The deck was not cleaned (for reasons of necessity which were obvious enough) and the coils and folds of rope were steeped in gore, as if in a slaughter-house. She was a fir built ship and her splinters had wounded nearly as many as the *Shannon's* shot. Pieces of skin and pendant hair were adhering to the sides of the ship; and in one place I noticed fingers protruding, as if thrust through the outer wall of the frigate; while several of the sailors to whom liquor had evidently been handed through the port-holes by visitors in boats, were lying asleep on the bloody floor, as if they had fallen in action and had expired where they lay.

Great honour was done to the victors. The Halifax merchants presented Broke

with an address and a piece of plate. The
home government promoted him, gave him
a pension, and made him a baronet. He
never entirely recovered from his wounds.
Aunt Susan Etter remembered the white
handkerchief he wore about his head in the
streets of Halifax. He quitted the service
and spent the afternoon of life as a country
gentleman, devoted to his family, tending
his estate, reading Horace, and going to
church. Incidentally, he underwent a formal court-martial for altering the equip-
ment of his ship. The second lieutenant,
the Halifax boy who brought the vessels
safely to port, who was never out of his
clothes and hardly slept during those six
critical days, became commander and rose
to be Sir Provo Wallis, Admiral of the
Fleet. He died in 1891, more than a hundred years old. Honour was also done to
the dead. Lawrence, who brought his ship
into action so 'handsomely,' as Broke wrote,
died of his wounds on the way to Halifax.
Haliburton saw his huge frame lying on
the quarter-deck of the *Chesapeake* with
the Stars-and-Stripes for a shroud. His
last words 'Don't give up the ship!' will
never be forgotten by his countrymen. On

Tuesday, June 8, his body was buried in old St. Paul's cemetery. 'His remains,' says Murdoch, 'were landed under a discharge of minute guns, at the King's Wharf, from whence they were followed to the grave by his own surviving officers, those of H.M. navy and army, and many respectable inhabitants of the town. On the American flag which covered the coffin was placed the sword, etc., of the deceased, and the pall was supported by six captains of the royal navy. A military band attended, and 300 men of the 64th regiment fired three volleys over the grave. The funeral service was performed by the rector of St. Paul's Church. Nothing could be more solemn and impressive than this procession, from its landing at the King's Wharf to the close.'

The lasting glory of the *Shannon* does not lie in the careful organisation of victory, nor in the success of her deadly onslaught, nor even in wiping the stain from the tarnished flag. It is found in the spirit of her commander, who obeyed 'the imperious call of honour.' Broke was a rich man, happily married; he might have spent his life in ease and comfort, but, 'Surely,' he wrote, 'no man deserves to enjoy an estate in England, who will not sacrifice some of his prospects, either by actual service, if possible, or at least by example of zeal and voluntary privation in her cause.'

IX

The *Saladin* Pirates

The 'Saladin' Pirates

O the left of the hospital drive at Halifax there is a low, round knoll encircled by a straggling fringe of young trees. I can never pass it without thinking of the story which ended there on the thirtieth of July, 1844. It is a black story of sordid crime, of blood and treasure, of punishment overtaking sin. Only he who told of the homicide on board of the *Flying Scud,* and the killings on Treasure Island could do it justice, but Tusitala sleeps on the top of Vaeea Mountain, and the chance auditor must do what he can lest the tale be lost.

In October 1842 Captain George Fielding sailed from Liverpool in the barque *Vitula,* a fine vessel of 460 tons, for Buenos Ayres. He was son of a soldier of the 30th Regiment and had lived in Gaspé. In person he was stout, well built, with strongly marked features, by no means unpleasing. His expression denoted great decision of character, a trait essential in the master of a ship. Although not an educated man, he had picked up enough French, Spanish, Portuguese, and Dutch to make himself understood in those languages among sea-faring folk. With him he took his son, George, a smart boy about fourteen years of age; and, though he had been married twice and his second wife was alive, he tried to persuade a girl in a Liverpool hotel to go off with him. Before he sailed, some agent of the Naval and Military Bible Society gave him a copy of the Holy Scriptures, suitably inscribed on the title page. It was little read, being reserved for another purpose.

Finding freights low at Buenos Ayres, Fielding sailed for Valparaiso. There the situation was no better, and he determined on a step which cost him his vessel. He sailed up the coast to the island of Chincha in order to smuggle a shipload of guano, the property of the Peruvian Government. The authorities got wind of this bold evasion of the law and sent a force of fifty soldiers to seize the *Vitula*. Fielding, undismayed, prepared to resist them; he had firearms laid out on the deck and was in the act of cutting the cable with a carving-knife, when the boat-load of Peruvians came alongside. His crew of fourteen, whom he bullied and starved, ran below, but Fielding and his mate fought. Fielding was shot in the shoulder, and was overpowered and brought with the *Vitula* to the port of Pisco, fourteen miles away. All the city came out to see him. He was so weak from the loss of blood, which saturated his clothing, and even his shoes, that he could not walk or stand. He was set on a mule and, with two men supporting him, was sent to the convent hospital to have his wounds dressed. From Pisco he was taken to Callao, and the *Vitula* was anchored under the guns of the fort. At first he was allowed the liberty of the port, although the crew were thrown into prison. Fielding, the resourceful, hatched a scheme for cutting out his vessel at midnight, and sounded various persons in the port on their willingness to help him. They informed on him, and he was put in prison. But with the help of his clever son, young George, he managed to escape in a poncho, passed the sentinel, and, after hiding in the shavings and carpenter's litter of a dockyard for two days and two nights, found refuge on board a British steamer and so reached Valparaiso once more.

He was, however, a ruined man. He had lost his vessel. The Peruvian courts had condemned and sold her for $15,000. How was he to face the owners, Myers & Company, Liverpool, whose vessel he had flung away? Who would ever employ him again? All he had managed to save from the wreck were some clothes, charts, and instruments, and also the ship's Bible. His son was not in custody and came to Valparaiso with him. All this happened in the month of July, 1843.

For some time Fielding remained in Valparaiso, trying to obtain a passage home. The *Jeremiah Garnett* and the *Belfast* would not take him, but Captain 'Sandy' Mackenzie, of the barque *Saladin,* of Newcastle, in an evil hour for himself, agreed to give Fielding and young George a free passage to London. The *Saladin* was a beautiful barque of about 550 tons register, with a bronze figurehead of a turbaned Turk, in accordance with her name; her cabin was magnificent, with staterooms suitable for lady passengers, fitted with mahogany and other valuable woods. She was loaded with guano and about twenty tons of copper. In her run, she carried thirteen bars of silver, each weighing 150 pounds, a chestful of dollars, and a number of money letters. The master was an old-fashioned, driving, swearing, drinking, capable son of Neptune. He had followed the sea for twenty years, had acquired a competence, and was now able to retire and live ashore. He had decided that this was to be his last voyage. His plan was to settle down at Newcastle with his family. On the 8th of February, 1844, the *Saladin* sailed from Valparaiso on what was to prove her last voyage. Including the two passengers, there were fourteen souls on board.

Apparently Mackenzie and Fielding were too much alike to get on well together. Two of a trade cannot agree, says the proverb. Before long, there were frequent quarrels between the two captains, with no assigned reason. On shipboard character manifests itself with surprising distinctness and rapidity. In a very short time, fellow passengers learn to like or dislike one another. The fact is notorious. These men soon came to hate each other, and quarrelled continually, even in the hearing of the crew. Fielding sometimes refused to come to the table for his meals, and Mackenzie would tell his mate, Bryerly, that it served him right for giving him a passage. Fielding was a desperate man, ruined, with no future, and, apparently from mingled motives of hatred and greed, formed a plot to get possession of the *Saladin.*

He first approached the sail-maker, George Jones, who came from County Clare. He was a man of middle size, with dark hair, full blue eyes, and heavy lowering brows. He was a cripple, having lost his leg by the fall of a spar, and, like long John Silver, he wore a stump. Until the Horn was rounded, Jones acted as steward, and was a witness of the endless quarrels between the captains in the splendid cabin. After rounding the Horn, a young Scotsman, named Galloway, took his place, a fresh-coloured boy of nineteen, with gray eyes and a prominent forehead. He was the son of a book-seller and he could read and write well; he even understood something of navigation. Jones went back to his sedentary sail-making, and Fielding, after his quarrels, would come and go all over them again with Jones. He would talk to the ignorant foremast hand about the amount of money on board, what a fine prize the *Saladin* would make, and asked if he would fight, if attacked by pirates, for such water-thieves were among the perils of ocean navigation as late as the forties. So he won Jones over, and then used him as a tool to gain the remainder of the mate's watch.

Another of the conspirators was William Trevaskiss, who had shipped under the name of Johnson. He was a short, broad-shouldered, thick-set man, with dark blue eyes, and in them a bold, determined, forbidding expression. According to his own account, he had been discharged from the U.S.S. *Constellation,* in Valparaiso, but he was more probably a deserter. To his shipmates he was 'Bill,' or 'the red-haired man.' The fourth conspirator was John Hazelton, five feet, six or seven inches in height, who claimed the North of Ireland as the place of his nativity. He was a black-haired man with neatly trimmed whiskers and large full bright eyes. According to one observer, he was 'the beau-ideal of a pirate,' which implies a standard of comparison. The fifth to join the murder pact

was Charles Gustavus Anderson, a Swede
from Udavalla, where his father was a master shipbuilder. He was about Hazelton's
height, dark-haired, brown-eyed, and he
spoke broken English. He was a mere lad,
only nineteen, but he entered into the plot
eagerly. When Jones broached it to him
and said that 'Sandy' was to be killed, the
Swede cried, 'By G—d, I'll take a knife and
cut his throat. He shall no more strike me
away from the helm.' All Fielding's tools
were young. The oldest was only twenty-
three.

Murder was brewing on the fated *Saladin,* but none except the conspirators had
the least inkling of what was coming. The
secret was well kept. Once peg-leg Jones
attempted to give the captain a hint, but
'Sandy' repulsed him with

'You d——d Irishman, I want to hear
nothing.'

After getting all one watch on his side,
Fielding played on their fears. Each man
must now help himself through, or his own
life would pay the forfeit. The leader's
plan was well considered, to the last detail.
It was to kill the captain and mate first,
then the members of the other watch, as

well as the cook and the steward; then, after gaining possession of the ship, they would sail her to some lonely harbour in Gaspé or Newfoundland, go back to the United States, return in a small vessel and carry off the dollars to spend in some foreign land. What was at the back of Fielding's brain can never be known, but from what he tried to do, it is doubtful if he ever intended that any of these ignorant tarpaulins should share in his gains.

The *Saladin* was two degrees north of the Line, in the region of calms and light baffling winds, by Friday, April 13th, and the plot was ripe. All but the sail-maker were on deck; and, as he was not there, the attempt was postponed. Jones tried to excuse himself for hanging back, but Fielding told him:

'There is no use making a fool of yourself. If you go back, your life is no more.'

On Saturday, Fielding and Mackenzie had a violent quarrel about the gig, which was heard by all the men on deck. Then Fielding told his accomplices,

'It must be done this night.'

That night, or rather, early Sunday morning, it was done. The mate, Bryerly, had the middle watch from midnight till four o'clock, and with him came on deck the four men engaged to kill him. He gave Hazelton the wheel, saying:

'Jack, steer the ship as well as you can. I do not feel very well.'

In the light airs anyone could steer. He went forward in his oil-skin coat and lay down on the hencoop. He had made his last entry in the log the day before at noon. Once he rose from the hencoop and asked Captain Fielding to go below. Fielding said he would, but first he went forward and spoke to the watch. Bryerly lay down on the coop again for his last sick slumber. The day before, the carpenter had been working on deck, and his tools, claw-hammer, broad-axe, maul, adze, and the rest lay in the stern of the long-boat. The four, Fielding, Trevaskiss, Jones, and Anderson crept aft silently and armed themselves from the carpenter's tools, and gathered around the unconscious mate. Trevaskiss brought down his axe; the unfortunate man had only time for a single cry, and Fielding, Trevaskiss, and Anderson bundled the body overside. Then Fielding came to Hazelton at the wheel:

'There is one gone,' he whispered.

Then followed an anxious, quavering time in the dark. The murderers were undecided what to do next. There were four of them, armed with lethal weapons, but they feared to attack Mackenzie single in his berth. They peered through the skylight into the after-cabin to see if he was asleep. At last the Swede and black-whiskered Hazelton stole down the companionway. There was a long silence. Jones, the shaking coward at the wheel, let the ship run up into the wind repeatedly in his agitation, and Fielding would take it out of his hands and put her back on her course. Then the two crept up the companionway again. They had done nothing. 'Sandy's' brown dog watched beside his master. He growled or stirred at their approach, and they were afraid he would bite them. In the silence of the tropical night the captain's bell rang twice, but no one attended to it. The *Saladin* made her quiet way through the broad waters.

They then decided to kill the carpenter, who lived in the steerage. Fielding stationed Trevaskiss, Hazelton, and the Swede around the hatch and called their victim up into the ambush. Before he reached the deck, Anderson struck him heavily with his own hammer. He fell forward stunned, or at least not killed outright. The three dragged him up and flung him over the side, but the water revived him and he made some outcry as he went astern. This gave Fielding the opportunity he wanted. Ambushing his murderers around the companion-way, he raised the cry of 'Man overboard.' At the same time, Jones rattled the skylight and joined in the cry. It brought the captain flying up the companion-way in his shirt, shouting to the steersman:

'Put the helm hard down!'

As his head came above the companion-way, Anderson, who was standing on the scuttle, struck him, but the blow injured him little. Mackenzie sprang at his assailant. Anderson ran to the break of the poop, then turned and grappled with his captain. Fielding shouted to Jones:

'D——n you, why don't you run after him. If you don't lay hold of him, I'll give you a clout that will kill you.'

Jones left the wheel and flung his arms around Mackenzie's neck. The luckless man had time to realise his plight and recognise his murderer. He cried, 'Oh, Captain Fielding—' when his charity passenger struck him twice with his broad-axe, saying:

'Oh, d——n you, I'll give it to you.'

Mackenzie fell to the deck. Fielding hauled the body forward of the companion-way and struck it again, and then flung it overboard. His son, young George, stood by shouting to 'give it to him.'

Three men killed! It was nerve-racking work, and more was to be done. Fielding, Hazelton, Anderson, and Trevaskiss went into the cabin to get a drink. Then the wooden-legged man was relieved at the wheel and he, too, went below for a supply of Dutch courage. When Fielding came on deck again, he said to his son:

'I am captain.'

Young George had regrets. He replied:

'It was a pity I had not a blow at Sandy.'

For some time the murderers stood on the quarter-deck consulting what to do next. There were still four lives to take. In order to arouse no suspicions, Fielding was to conceal himself in the companion-way. Young George was behind him at the foot of the ladder, armed with a carving-knife, under his father's orders to 'stick' the first man who should come down. Jones was to lie down in the long-boat, Anderson was to lean against the main-mast pretending to be asleep, while Hazelton and Trevaskiss should go to call the morning watch. The plan succeeded to admiration.

There was a pretence of hauling down the flying-jib and the captain's watch was called. It was Jem Allen's trick at the wheel. When the sleepy man came aft to relieve Hazelton, he paused for a moment and stood facing the stern, for a reason all sailors will understand. Nothing was further from his thoughts than death, when Anderson stole up behind and struck him in the back of the head with an axe. The force of the blow sent the man overboard, Fielding watching all the while from the shadow of the companion-way. Then he said to Hazelton, relieving him at the wheel:

'Jack, you have done nothing yet. Take that axe!'

The order, as Hazelton stated afterwards, was 'strict,' and, as he was afraid of being killed, he obeyed. Thomas Moffat came sleepily and unsuspiciously on deck and sat down on a spar near the galley, with his two good shipmates, Hazelton and Trevaskiss, on each side of him. As Moffat turned his head toward the bow, Trevaskiss nodded to Hazelton to strike. He struck with the axe; and Trevaskiss struck; and Moffat fell to the deck bleeding like a stuck pig. A third seaman, Samuel Collins, had gone into the head as look-out. After felling Moffat, Hazelton sang out to Anderson to 'finish' Collins. One blow in the skull 'finished' him, and he sank through the rigging to the sea.

Six men murdered within an hour or so! In all the seven seas that peaceful Sunday morning was there a stranger ship afloat than the elegant *Saladin,* rocking in the doldrums! Again and again her deck had been the scene of murder most foul, and, through it all two men had slept the heavy sleep of tired sailors. These were the cabin-boy, Galloway, and William Carr, the cook, a stocky, pock-marked, fresh-coloured Englishman from North Shields, who could read and write and carried a well-worn pocket Bible. They also were marked for death,

223

and Fielding, the resolute, was all for having them go the way of the others; but his butchers were sick of their bloody work and would not consent to their shipmates' death. Perhaps it was the daylight, which showed them what they had done.

About six o'clock, Carr awoke and turned out to his duty as usual. Like Bryerly, he had been sick for a couple of days. As he came aft to the galley, he saw on the starboard side by the foremast backstay a great quantity of blood, where poor Moffat had been felled like an ox. On the poop stood Fielding and his four accomplices. The helmsman had called them up from the cabin when he saw Carr on deck. The cook was slow to realize what had happened, and came farther aft to inquire the reason for the blood, when Fielding bade him halt.

'What is the matter?' Carr asked in confusion.

'Come up. We will not harm you.' Carr came up the ladder crying like a child with fear, and asked again. 'What is the matter?'

'I am commander of this vessel now.'

'What does this mean?'

'The master and crew have gone away and left us,' replied Fielding.

Carr glanced around the empty sea and then at the *Saladin's* deck. All the boats were in their places.

'It is impossible,' he gasped. 'It can't be the case—all the boats are about the ship.'

Fielding then spoke out.

'We have finished Sandy. We shall have no more cursing and swearing now. We have finished the carpenter, mate, and Jemmy, Moffat, and Sam.'

Carr looked down at the feet of the murderers and saw their bloody tools, recognizing a small hatchet of his own, and the carpenter's adze, maul, and hammer, and he thought he was within a hair's-breadth of his death. Amid his tears and sobs, he managed to stammer:

'It is a serious circumstance.'

Said Fielding: 'Will you join us?'

'If I do not,' said poor Carr, 'I suppose I must go the same road as the rest.'

The sailors sang out that he should not go overboard. Hazelton made the trembling man sit down on the skylight and tried to quiet him. No more lives were to be taken, and, disappointed, Fielding told him to go down into the cabin for some grog. Young George gave him something

out of a bottle, which he needed badly to
steady his nerves, and then he went forward to light the galley fire and prepare
breakfast.   Nearly all that day he was crying for fear.   Well he might.   As soon as
his b'ack was turned, Fielding told his tools
that when they got near land he would kill
these two and the 'Dutchman.'   Galloway,
the cabin-boy, had followed Carr on deck
laughing, and, when he learned of the murders, wished that he could have had a 'cut
at Sandy.'   He agreed to share the lot of the
pirates.

The ship was put about, and Fielding
shaped the course northwest and by north,
away from London, and towards Newfoundland.   The remnant of the crew were
divided into watches, Carr, Galloway, and
Hazelton forming one.   After breakfast,
Fielding spent the morning rummaging the
papers, letter-bags, and desks in the after-
cabin.   A number of money letters were
burnt by his orders, after the money en-
closed had been taken from them.   He
locked the spirits from the men, and it was
observed that he drank heavily himself.
Even his iron nerves needed artificial
strength.   There were some arms on

board, and these the crew threw overboard, except a cutlass and Captain Mackenzie's fowling-piece, which Fielding said they might need to shoot sea-birds. Their butchering tools, two hatchets, the carpenter's broad-axe, adze, and large hammer also went over the side, 'lest,' said Captain Fielding, 'we should get jealous of one another.'

Being the Christian Sabbath, the day was not allowed to pass without some form of religious observance. Fielding called the crew into the fine, mahogany-fitted cabin, where they had spliced the main-brace that morning and boasted, as the liquor took hold, which was the best murderer. He explained that it was best for all to swear 'to be brotherly together;' and he brought out his Bible, which had shared his adventures from Liverpool round the Horn and back again thus far, and which he had preserved when he lost the *Vitula*. In turn, each blood-guilty man kissed the book and swore to be 'loyal and brotherly' to the rest. So did Fielding, who was even then plotting the murder of the men he was swearing to fidelity. His son was not required to take the oath, being too young.

One thinks of the homicides on the deck of the *Flying Scud,* repeating the Lord's Prayer in unison.

The murder plot had been a complete success. The ship, with all its wealth, was in the hands of Fielding and his assassins; but a black atmosphere of suspicion descended at once upon that fatal and perfidious barque. That same night, Trevaskiss told Carr and Galloway that Fielding meant to do for them, and that if they went he would lose his life as well. So these three formed some sort of pact, an offensive-defensive alliance. When Trevaskiss went below at eight o'clock, the end of his watch, he found that, by the captain's orders, Carr and Galloway were to berth forward in the forecastle, while all the rest were to live in the cabin. He asked his mates why the cook and the cabin-boy were not allowed the same privileges? He was referred to the new captain, and Fielding answered:

'We can't trust them.'

'If you are afraid, I am not,' said Trevaskiss, 'and if they sleep in the forecastle, so will I.'

He carried his point. All shared the same quarters. Fielding's scheme to divide the

men and finish them in detail was thwarted.
He had foolishly told Trevaskiss that he
would poison Carr and Galloway when they
got near land. He also approached Galloway and Anderson separately to help to
get rid of the others.

On Monday there was a division of Mackenzie's clothes and effects. Carr and Fielding had a difference over a pair of new
trousers, which the captain wanted for his
son. In the afternoon, they set the fore-
topmast stunsail. At six, all hands had tea
in the cabin, after which Carr set some
bread in the galley, returned to the cabin
and lay down in one of the beds until he
should be called to take his turn at the
wheel, at eight. While there, Fielding came
down, took the cabin light into the pantry
and muffled it with the tablecloth. Then
he went into the after-cabin. What he was
doing there Carr could not make out, but,
from the sounds, it seemed that he was
loading the fowling-piece. He was capable
of any treachery. The Bible oath, and
Fielding's cure for 'jealousy,' did not prove
completely efficacious.

When Carr went on deck, the rest of the
hands came down into the cabin. Then en-

sued a turbulent, confused, wrangling scene
that lasted for hours. Under the cabin-
table, Trevaskiss had previously discovered
two horse-pistols. Everybody thought that
all the arms had been thrown overboard,
except the fowling-piece. Now Hazelton
drew the pistols out of their hiding-place
and said:

'These mean something. Who put them
there?'

Everyone denied all knowledge of them.

There was a further search for weapons.
In the locker, a large copper canister full of
powder was discovered, and in the spirit-
locker, of which Fielding had the key, the
carving-knife which had been missing since
Sunday. In the locker were also two bottles
of brandy, which, from the taste, the sailors
thought were poisoned. All these were
taken on deck with the fowling-piece and
thrown over the side. Fielding denied all
knowledge of the knife and tried to turn
the men from their purpose by the offer of
grog; but they now realised that it was their
life or his, and they were not to be denied.
Fielding threatened and stormed. He told
them, what was the truth, that they were
all afraid of him, and, at last, he tried to

regain the deck. He said he would throw himself overboard, and turned to the door. Then they fell on him and bound him hand and foot, he screaming, shouting, daring them to kill him. At last they gagged him, and in that condition he passed the night in the cabin under constant guard, while the hands consulted how to dispose of him. Hazelton was for confining him in the forecastle and putting him ashore the first land they made. Carr said he could never sleep while Fielding lived. But the four others declared they would not lend a hand to another man's death as long as they were in the ship. It was a long wrangle in the cabin of that fated vessel, while Fielding, gagged and tied hand and foot, sat helpless and heard it all. In those long hours he must have savoured all the bitterness of death.

That night no one slept in the *Saladin*. Fear reigned. The sailors dreaded that their tyrant might get free. They kept the boy from his father lest he should help him. So the watches passed, till the dawn of Tuesday, the seventeenth of April. The morning brought counsel. About seven, Fielding's feet were unbound and he was brought on deck. By this time the liquor must have died out of him; he must have understood that his last hour had come. Even now, he was not at the end of his resources. He begged Galloway, who was at the wheel, to cast him loose and he would save his life a second time. Then the four most deeply dyed in blood, Jones, Hazelton, Anderson, and Trevaskiss, decided that Carr and Galloway, the two who had as yet 'done nothing,' must share their guilt by killing Fielding. Galloway refused, but the others compelled him to touch their baffled leader. Carr and Jones carried him aft and heaved him into the sea.

It takes about four minutes to drown . . . .

Then Carr and Galloway seized young George and put him overside, at the larboard gangway. He screamed and tore their clothes and clung to them. They shook him off . . . .

The others sat about the deck and watched both scenes.

After this they got at the liquor, and every day some of the crew were drunk. They made Galloway navigator, as he had the most education, and he kept the reckoning in a memorandum book. But, as the old ballad of the *Saladin* runs:

> We mostly kept before the wind,
> For we could do no more.

They lived at rack and manger in the cabin. They threw some of the copper overboard to lighten the ship, and some they used to sink the gig. They nailed a board over the name on the stern, and they painted the bronze Turk at bow white, clumsy expedients to conceal the identity of the vessel. They planned to scuttle her and escape with the dollars in the one remaining boat, but they waited just a little too long.

On the morning of the 22nd of May, the *Saladin,* with all sails set, even to her royals, drove hard on the island at the mouth of Country Harbour, Nova Scotia, at a place ever since called Saladin Point.

On hearing that a large vessel was ashore, Captain Cunningham, of the schooner *Billow,* manned his boat and went to her assistance. He found everything in the greatest confusion on board, the disorder in the cabin being especially offensive to his sailorly eye. He stood by for thirty-six hours putting things to rights. The sailors, honest fellows, had a plausible story about their captain dying at sea and the mate and several hands being washed off the yard. Since then, they had lived rather freely. But their stories did not agree very well. There were instruments belonging to a Captain Fielding, who, they said, had died at Valparaiso. The last entry in the log was for the fourteenth of April. Suspicion grew, and, in the end, the six honest sailormen were arrested and brought to Halifax in H.M.S. *Fair Rosamond*. The poor, mishandled *Saladin* became a total wreck, but the value of the silver, copper, and dollars salved from her and deposited in the Bank of Nova Scotia was £18,000. Perhaps it was as well that the *Saladin* went to pieces, for none would ever want to sail in that death-ship again.

There was a legal difficulty to overcome. Crime had plainly been committed, but it had been committed on the high seas outside the jurisdiction of any Nova Scotian court. So a special court was constituted, in which the Admiral of the station sat as judge in all the splendour of full naval uniform beside the Chief-justice, and three puisne judges. Legal formalities were hardly needed, for, while in their cells in the old penitentiary on the Arm, Carr and Galloway sent for a lawyer and made a clean breast of their share in the murders. They likewise confessed the crimes of their shipmates, which they did not witness, as they were below and asleep at the time. Carr's statement is clear, coherent, and brief, showing decided intelligence. No doubt all hands had discussed the sequence of events and the various details many times. The confessions of Jones, Trevaskiss, Hazelton, and Anderson followed, almost as a matter of course. To find them guilty and sentence them to death was the only course open to the court. The plea was changed from piracy, which involved hanging in chains, to plain murder, and they were sentenced all four to be hanged by the neck until they were dead. Carr and Galloway were also tried for the murder of the two Fieldings; but the plea was made that they were forced to do the deed by their shipmates, and so they were acquitted.

The execution was a public spectacle long remembered in Halifax. The South Common was bare of buildings then, except for

the little chapel 'Built-in-a-day' standing in
the Catholic cemetery. On the small eminence opposite, the scaffold was erected. At
each end of the platform was an upright
post, and a stout beam, from which dangled four nooses, joined them. The four
'drops,' were held in place by simple wood-
en 'buttons,' controlled by a single cord.
One pull of the cord opened the four trap-
doors simultaneously.

Early on the 30th of July, a company of
the 52nd Foot formed a circle round the
scaffold and kept the spectators at a proper
distance. All the city turned out to see the
sight. About ten o'clock a procession
came along Tower Road; first the sheriff in
a gig, then the four murderers in two closed
carriages. Three Catholic priests attended
the two Irishmen, and an Anglican clergy-
man, Trevaskiss and the Swede. On each
side marched a strong body of the First
Royals, with fixed bayonets. The four
condemned men mounted the platform and
took their places on the four trap-doors.
They took farewell of one another and
shook hands. Jones kissed his fellows on
the cheek and said a few words to the crowd
to the effect that he was an Irishman from

Clare, that he was sorry for what he had done, and that he hoped for pardon from God. Imprisonment had taken the sailors' tan from their cheeks, they looked 'debilitated,' but 'placid.' Anderson alone seemed unconcerned and looked over the heads of the crowd to the blue, sparkling sea. Hazelton and Jones handed their written confessions to their spiritual advisers. The priests knelt in prayer, the control cord was pulled, and the four men dropped to their death. In three-quarters of an hour the bodies were cut down. Hazelton and Jones were buried in the Catholic cemetery; but Trevaskiss and Anderson were inearthed in the paupers' burying-ground. Anderson was dug up and anatomised by a certain young doctor, and his skull may be seen to this day in the provincial museum.

This is the tragedy of the *Saladin*. Of the fourteen persons who sailed in her from Valparaiso on the eighth of February, 1844, only two remained alive on the thirtieth of July. In all the annals of the sea, there is scarce a record of more revolting crime.

Of these two survivors, Galloway disappeared, but Carr, according to local tradition, settled down in Digby county and died there not very long ago. He had noted peculiarities. For one thing he rarely walked, but always went at a 'shepherd's trot.' He was a very respectable man, a pillar of a local church, but once a year on the anniversary of his crime he drowned remembrance in liquor.

Ballads were made on the affair which still cling to the memory of Nova Scotians. The blood-stained hatch was long preserved in the museum, but has recently disappeared. The *Saladin's* cabin windows were built into a carpenter's shop in Country Harbour, and some people believe that pirate treasure may yet be found where the fatal vessel went ashore.

X

The *Sarah* Stands By

The 'Sarah' Stands By

N the month of January, 1850, the city of New York went wild over a plain master-mariner from Yarmouth, Nova Scotia. Wall Street, the Mayor and Corporation, the press, the ladies and the populace of Gotham showered attentions upon him. He excited the interest of even such august bodies as the Senate of the United States and the House of Representatives. His fame extended far beyond the bounds of America. 'Solid pudding' as well as 'empty praise' were his in no stinted measure; and then he went his way, and New York knew him no more. The excitement passed and is forgotten as well as the reason for it; but the memory of brave deeds well done should not be allowed to perish from the world for lack of a faithful chronicler. This is the tale of two ships and two captains; one of the captains was a man.

The saga begins in the river Mersey, on October 23rd, 1849, with the sailing of the smart American packet-ship *Caleb Grimshaw* from Liverpool for New York. Grimshaw is an old Liverpool name. A Robert Grimshaw was captain of the *Spy* privateer in 1757. Caleb Grimshaw & Co. was a Quaker firm of ship's agents; the head of it used 'thou' and 'thee' in a letter of remonstrance to *The Times,* of which more anon. Evidently this vessel had been named out of compliment to him when she was built two years before in a famous New York ship-yard; and she belonged to the firm of Samuel Thompson & Nephew. A new, able, well-found ship, she represented the last word in naval architecture, used as a model for the class praised by Dickens in *American Notes* as 'The noble American vessels which have made their packet service the finest in the world.' Her captain was William E. Hoxie, who had been in the service for twenty years, reputed as both competent and trustworthy. He was a teetotaller himself and sailed his ship on temperance principles. His eldest son, twenty-two years of age, sailed with him as first mate; and he had his wife and a younger

child on board. An American packet of
this day measured about a thousand tons;
and, between decks, with the rudest accommodations, this particular vessel carried
427 steerage passengers, one hundred of
whom had only a month to live. Some
modern steamers of ten thousand tons do
not carry more. It was immediately after
the cruel famine years, and the Irish were
fleeing from their own stricken land in
thousands and in tens of thousands. In the
cabin were six first-class passengers. One
of them was an unknown Englishman who
had the gift of putting down in plain words
what he saw taking place under his own
eyes. This nameless eye-witness is the
chief authority for the tale; he lived through
it. The *Grimshaw* carried a steward, a
stewardess and a doctor. Her crew consisted of eighteen men with four mates over
them. Stowed below was a general cargo
valued at half a million dollars. There were
also one hundred tons of iron and between
six and seven hundred tons of coal on the
floor of the hold. To save passengers and
crew in case of accident, the *Grimshaw*
had only four boats, one at the stern, one on
each quarter, with the long-boat in its usual

berth amidships; but these were considered an adequate provision. No vessel of the time carried more.

In the days of sail, there was a great difference in crossing the Western Ocean, according as the passage was eastward or westward. From America, the prevailing winds might rush a vessel across in fifteen days. Coming back from Liverpool to New York was another story. Head winds and calms often prolonged the voyage westward into weeks and even months. Sometimes an emigrant ship took a hundred days from port to port. The *Caleb Grimshaw* had the usual luck of west-bound packets. By November 11th she was only about half way across. To be exact, her position was 37W., 41N., which means that she was practically on the same parallel as New York and headed for her port of destination. Although it was winter, the neighborhood of the Gulf Stream made the weather mild. The nearest land was Flores in the Azores, four hundred miles to the eastward. Sunday the 11th was memorable because, for the first time in almost three weeks, the *Grimshaw* had a favorable wind, and Captain Hoxie was able to set his studding-sails. Night came on. Though favorable, the wind was light and the *Grimshaw* with every stitch of canvas set, drifted along at the rate of two knots an hour. The emigrants were all below in their berths, when, about nine o'clock, smoke began to pour out of the fore-hatch. Without a moment's warning, the calamity most dreaded by sailors had befallen the crowded emigrant ship,—fire at sea.

At the cry of 'Fire!' the shouted orders and turmoil on deck, panic terror seized the steerage. Well it might! Only the year before, the *Ocean Monarch* just out of Liverpool was burnt to the water's edge and 178 of her 399 passengers perished. That horror was fresh in all minds. Now the terrified men, women and children poured up from below, and rushed to the quarter-deck, the seat of authority, wildly imploring the captain to save their lives. Kneeling, lying down on the deck in the dark, drowning the officers' orders with shrieks of entreaty, the hapless emigrants made almost impossible the measures most needed for their safety. Some of them never reached the deck, but were suffocated by the smoke in their berths. Through the howling crowd, the officers managed to fight their way to the fore-hatch, the point of danger. On the forecastle just above it was a large force-pump used for washing the decks. Two minutes after the alarm, it was manned and pouring a copious stream of water into the steerage. This force-pump, as the ship's agents afterwards insisted truly, was the means of saving the ship, for the time being. First and last, it flooded the ship nine feet deep. Fire-buckets supplemented the pump. Tons of sea water pumped into the *Grimshaw* sank her deeper in the water, and almost destroyed her stability, but they did not touch the heart of the fire. Still the thick black smoke poured up from the fore-hatch through the sails and rigging to mingle with the black night.

After an hour of terrific exertion, with pump-brakes and buckets, the emigrants' quarters between decks were fairly well flooded; and still the smoke poured up the fore-companion-way. It was plain that the fire was not in the steerage but deeper down, in the lower hold. One of the lower hatches was lifted by men stifling in the smother, and choking volumes of thick smoke poured up. The nozzle of the hose from the force-pump was directed down the hatch-way, fresh hands were put on the pump-brakes, but the fire was not checked. It only produced clouds of steam; and the heat was almost intolerable. 'No human being could breathe between decks' said Captain Hoxie. Then young Hoxie volunteered to go down and discover, if possible, where the fire was. In a bowline, he was let down into the inferno of swift suffocation; but he was hardly below the combings, when he sang out, and was drawn up, almost insensible. In the few seconds he had seen the lower hold ablaze on both sides of the ship, abaft the chain-locker.

His report must have spread throughout the ship as swiftly as the fire itself. Panic intensified. Order and discipline came to an abrupt end. While the captain's back was turned and he and his officers were battling with the fire, there was a rush for safety towards the stern of the ill-fated ship. Some of the passengers indeed volunteered to help the crew at the back-breaking, breathless labor of pumping, but others had to be driven out from among the women and children where they lay groaning and crying. Some others attempted to launch the port quarter-boat hanging from the davits. Clumsy and panic-stricken, they succeeded only in swamping her and drowning twelve of their number alongside. Panic spread to the crew of 'packet rats.' The man at the wheel deserted his post. He and the boatswain, the second cook and several of the sailors put compasses, water and provisions in the stern boat, lowered her without mishap, got in, and remained there in comparative safety for several days, towing behind the burning ship, and ready in an instant to cut the painter. They at least were provided for; passengers and messmates could shift for themselves.

If the emigrants had only hindered the movements of the officers and crew, if they had only hung back instead of helping with the pumps and buckets, the harm they did would have been negative. In their witless terror, they did far worse. They stove in the two huge water-tanks on deck holding 1100 gallons apiece and poured the contents down the hatchway. This is when a little pistolling would have prevented far worse trouble later on, but Captain Hoxie and his mates were unable to prevent the suicidal work of destruction. Still the force-pump clanked on and the bucket brigade was more thoroughly organised. This gave an opportunity for some of the crew to take in almost all sail and heave the vessel aback. Towards two o'clock on the Monday morning, the smoke seemed to be less in volume, the wild wailing and uproar died away, for the worn-out passengers had fallen asleep on the hard deck wherever they could find a clear space, with only a few planks between them and the raging fire. Henceforward, they had to endure hunger and thirst as well as exposure and terror. All provisions were below, and could not be got at without opening the hatches. Opening the hatches would mean the ship ablaze. Only by keeping air from the flames was there any hope of escaping swift destruction. Some of the emigrants did not taste a drop of water for ten days.

Monday was a day of comparative calm, after the wild turmoil of Sunday night. When daylight came, a certain amount of order was restored. The starb'oard quarter-boat was lowered and three men ordered into her to keep her free. The port quarter-boat was baled out and three more sailors detailed to her. The stern boat remained towing with her occupants. These were plainly preparations for abandoning the ship. Any one on board with a knowledge of arithmetic must have marvelled how three, or even four, boats could possibly save over four hundred and fifty persons. Eyewitness thought they might have accommodated one out of every ten. About nine o'clock, the long-boat was hoisted out and passed astern. Mrs. Hoxie and the child were lowered into it from the state-room windows, and the six cabin passengers followed. One was an old lady. Compasses, charts, oars and provisions were also put in. Now all four boats were streamed astern. One of the mid-ship pumps was got to work, and the sailors began to build a raft.

The scene at the after end of the *Grimshaw* must have been heartrending. Eyewitness calls it 'painful in the extreme. Some of the passengers rushed to the captain's stateroom, beseeching him to save them; numbers crowded round the stern where the second mate was lowering the ladies into the long-boat; others were at prayers, while mothers and children, husbands and wives embraced each other and mingled their tears together.'

Their fears were well founded. Before Eyewitness got into the long-boat, the cabin floor was quite warm, and smoke was sifting through the seams of the deck. Two girls lowered themselves into the water by a rope hanging over the stern, although they were told they could not be taken into any of the boats. Still they clung together until nearly exhausted, when room was made for them in the long-boat.

Late in the afternoon came the abdication of the captain. One of the oldest rules in the rigid code of the sea prescribes that the captain shall be the last man to leave the ship. It holds good from the proudest dreadnought to the humblest fishing-smack. Rarely is it disregarded. But on Monday, November 12th, Captain William E. Hoxie betook himself to the long-boat, amid wild Irish shrieks of

'Oh, Captain dear! Save us! Save us!'

He assured his frenzied passengers that he would stay by them to the last, but his assurance gave them cold comfort.

The results of the captain's abdication were seen at once. So far as wind and weather were concerned, the situation remained unchanged. All Monday and Tuesday, the *Grimshaw* 'lay to' on a heaving, windless sea, with her four boats towing astern and the fire eating deeper into her entrails. On Monday, before the captain quitted his command, the sailors had constructed three rafts and hoisted one over the side. It was rigged with a mast and a small sail; and it was supplied with a barrel of pork, a barrel of beef, a little water, but no bread. Some twenty of the more energetic and more desperate among the emigrants got on it, and, fearing that it would be overcrowded, cut the line which held it to the ship. Away it drifted before the wind to the eastward, to be swallowed up in the void.

Others of the emigrants were affected in a different way by the desertion of their official guardian. The instinct of plunder awoke. There must have been muttered plotting on the Monday, for, when night fell, desperate men rushed the cabins, broke into all the trunks and boxes they could find and rifled them, just as the stewards of the *Scotsman* went through the staterooms, slashing open the passengers' luggage when

she was wrecked in the Straits of Belle Isle.
American packets were navigated on coffee,
fore and aft, not rum.   Perhaps the raiders
were looking for food as well as spoil.   At
any rate, they found two cases of brandy
and a few bottles of wine, not the property
of the ship, but of the cabin passengers. The
liquor drove the hungry men stark mad,
and hell broke loose on the pitch-dark,
filthy, crowded deck of the doomed *Grimshaw*. The only hope of saving the ship
and the lives of all on board lay with young
Hoxie and the loyal remnant of the crew,
who still stood by him; and the homicidal
maniacs got hold of two guns and tried to
kill them.   Hoxie and his trusties met them
with their bare fists. They overpowered
the howling lunatics who carried loaded
guns, wrenched them out of their hands
and flung them into the sea. They armed
themselves with pistols and bowie-knives
and 'kept the infuriated savages at bay,' until the brandy died out of them, and they
sank down exhausted. All through this
riot in the dark, while young Hoxie and his
loyal followers were fighting for their lives,
not a man in the towing boats lifted a hand
to help them.   How long the riot lasted is

not known, but at last it came to an end, and once more the peace of utter weariness settled down on the burning ship and her human stye.

An American 'bucko' mate is a hard man to kill. On Tuesday morning, young Hoxie came off in one of the boats with some provisions and a small tin of water for his father and the other occupants of the long-boat. He reported a terrible night.

Tuesday the 13th passed quietly. The boats brought off some mattresses and leaves of the cabin table, which were laid along the bottom of the crowded long-boat. She was so leaky, and shipped so much water that two men were kept baling, day and night. Evidently the long-boat had made many voyages secured amidships upside-down and was no longer seaworthy.

On Wednesday the 14th, the wind blew fair for the Azores, but the *Grimshaw* remained stationary. In the afternoon, the crew found a barrel of flour, and during the night of the 14th-15th, one man on board the *Grimshaw* did his duty, the first cook. All night he was busy in the galley baking. Captain and Mrs. Hoxie and all in the long-boat had been subsisting uncomfortably enough on 'cake, pickles and cheese taken from the cabin.' They found a cask of the cook's fresh bread very welcome.

About nine o'clock this morning, the crew made sail on the *Grimshaw*. Still burning, with nine feet of water in her hold, the smoke still coming up the forward hatch, she went lurching off vaguely in the direction of New York. This was an error in judgment, plain even to the intelligence of cabin passengers; and it was due to Captain Hoxie, who still seems to have exercised control from his refuge in the towing long-boat. Like the Duke of Plaza-Toro, he led his regiment from behind. When night came on, the *Grimshaw* was hove-to by his orders; for the long-boat was in danger of swamping. An old sail-cover was passed out from the ship and nailed over the boat like a tent or awning. It kept the seas from breaking over the side. On Thursday, at the entreaties of the mates and the crew, Captain Hoxie allowed the course of the *Grimshaw* to be altered, and she was headed for the Azores. By noon she had run eighty or ninety miles to the eastward recovering lost distance; and at night she was again hove-to.

17

On Friday, at dawn, the hard-worked remnant of the crew made sail again. About nine o'clock, it fell calm and the cabin passengers wearied with their cramped quarters, misery and constant danger in the long-boat, 'where we had lain four days and nights side by side without being able to change our positions and completely wet through,' got back into the ship. Captain Hoxie remained where he was. An hour later, the look-out sighted a dim shape wavering on the far horizon,—a sail! It meant reviving hope to all on board; it might mean rescue and life preserved in dire extremity. The course of the *Grimshaw* was altered in order to cross the stranger's track; but there was little wind and progress was slow. To try and overtake her, the second mate put off in one of the boats, with five hands. They had a long, hard row which lasted till nightfall. All eyes on the *Grimshaw* were turned towards the strange and indifferent ship, with what hopes and fears. At the end of two hours more, they were able to distinguish the rig and course of the distant vessel. She was a barque standing west by north, on the road to America and away

from the Azores. For two hours more the
Grimshaw followed her, till hope of rescue
was as good as dead. It seemed as if the
stranger meant to avoid the ship in distress,
and young Hoxie put his vessel on her
former course eastward. But keen eyes
were watching the manoeuvre from the
stranger's deck. As the *Grimshaw* came
about some one on board the distant barque
spied the Stars-and-Stripes fluttering, union
down, in her main rigging. Until that minute, the flag was invisible from the
stranger's deck. No doubt it was the captain himself who read the signal of distress
through his big brass telescope, which he
was destined to put to a very different use.
Instantly he wore ship and began to follow
the *Grimshaw* to the eastward. Hope revived. In an hour's time, she was near
enough to speak and give young Hoxie
necessary information in the curt speech of
the sea;—*Sarah*,—of Yarmouth—Nova
Scotia—Cook, master—timber ship—in ballast—from London—homeward b o u n d—
will stand by; and the first mate barked back
the plight of the *Grimshaw*. Cook directed
him to keep the *Sarah* company. Both vessels would burn lights to guide each other.

So they stood on together to the eastward.

The master of the *Sarah*, David Cook, was a typical Yarmouth County skipper. For three generations, the Cooks had followed the sea. Ephraim the grandfather came to Yarmouth in 1762. He was the first Englishman in the country, and, though he lost a leg as a young man, he sailed vessels and founded the fishing industry in that part of the province. To the Yarmouth children, he was *the* Captain Cook who had *not* perished in the Pacific. And Ephraim begat Caleb and Manasseh; and Caleb begat Caleb the second, and David, our hero, and Nehemiah and Amos. The Cook pedigree reads like a chapter in Genesis. In all, there were four-and-twenty master mariners of this one stirp. Are not their names written in the book of the Chronicles of Yarmouth by George S. Brown? The Cooks were men of tried ability, for fools and weaklings do not rise to the command of ships. David Cook was a tall, handsome, athletic, young man, not long married. In this crisis he proved true to the splendid traditions of a sea-faring race.

After the five days of merciful calms and

light airs, a change of weather was due. Captain Cook prepared for the emergency by shortening sail. He took in his courses and top-gallant sails, and double-reefed his topsails. The expected gale came. That night it blew hard with frequent squalls. Before night fell, however, the *Sarah* had picked up the second mate's boat, and taken the sailors out of one of the quarter-boats. Captain Hoxie, his wife and child, the steward, stewardess and doctor were also rescued from the miserable, leaky long-boat, though they had a narrow escape from drowning while getting on board the *Sarah* in the dusk of the stormy November day. The wind and sea were getting up. It was impossible to take any more persons off. Eyewitness was among those who remained on board the *Grimshaw* in the night of terror which followed.

That the *Sarah* was proceeding under storm canvas shows what she expected. The emigrant ship followed as best she could, at a slower pace. The three boats towing astern were swamped and lost; and the stern was dragged out of the rotten long-boat. Weighted down with the nine feet of water in her hold, the *Grimshaw* rolled and wallowed frightfully in the heavy sea. When she rolled to one side, the tons of water below would hold her down on that side for minutes that would seem ages. Then she would recover slowly; and the sickening roll to the other side would begin. At every roll, the deck must have been almost at right angles to the plane of the sea. And this rolling continued all night. Eyewitness says,

'Every moment we expected to go down; the ship rolled in a frightful manner, dipping her studding-sail booms quite under water, while at every roll, the seas came in on the quarter-deck and even into the wheel-house.'

These restrained words express faintly the feelings of the cabin passengers on the quarter-deck. The terror of the three hundred poor creatures, men, women and children, half-naked, drenched, famished, parched, exhausted, unsheltered on the main deck can be imagined. Holding on to whatever they could clutch, for dear life, they must have been flung from side to side, into the scuppers, the whole night long. And among them were at least two expectant mothers, whose time was near.

They could feel the whole deck working under them, six inches each way, at every roll. The whole interior of the hull was on fire. No one knew when the flames might burst out. To make their despair complete, about three o'clock in the morning, they lost the faint twinkle of the *Sarah's* lights. On board the *Grimshaw,* there was not an aid to navigation left, no chart, compass, sextant, chronometer; but somehow, by some seaman instinct, young Hoxie managed to navigate his vessel and keep her on her course. She was a new vessel, and must have been staunch and well rigged to survive such a racking. Some principle of buoyancy kept her afloat, and she lived through that night. When the long expected dawn came, the anxious watchers in the *Grimshaw* saw to their great joy, the faithful *Sarah* five or six miles ahead, pitching and tossing on the stormy sea.

Still they misjudged her, not knowing Captain David Cook. They thought he was going to desert them, as the barque sailed on ahead and made no sign. Nothing was farther from the master's mind. About two o'clock, the sea had somewhat abated, and the *Sarah* was hove-to. Two hours later, the *Grimshaw* came up with her friend in need, and also hove-to. And now another Yarmouth man comes into the saga, James Coward, first mate of the *Sarah*. The surname is a mistake; never was a more complete misnomer. The captain's place is always on board his own ship; he is the directing will, and the first mate is his chief executive to put the captain's will into effect. Courage is assumed as a first axiom, and taken as a matter of course. He cannot do his work without it. Like that mirror of all seamen, Francis Drake, the first mate is 'first at every turn where courage, skill and industry are wont to be employed.' Now under James Coward's direction, the *Sarah's* two boats were lowered, pulled over to the waiting *Grimshaw*, loaded with their human freight, and conveyed safely to the deck of the rescue ship. It was a task calling for cool judgment, swift action and professional skill. Women and children came first, for that is another ancient rule of the sea. To get them safely over the side of a rolling vessel into a small boat pitching and tossing alongside is no easy task. But

Coward and his men did it. With the male
emigrants there was no special problem;
they could let themselves down by means
of ropes. This women could not do, lack-
ing the strength and the nerve; they had
to be lowered in slings. Rescuing the
children was harder still, for neither
method was applicable to them. But trust
sailors for ingenuity. The sixty-one children and the six small babies were done up
in bags and so passed down the side of the
Grimshaw and up the side of the *Sarah*.
One of the marvels of this tale is the saving alive of so many children. Between
three o'clock and dark, the *Sarah's* two
boats transhipped one hundred and thirty-
three persons, including most of the women
and children, without a single mishap.
Amongst them were the cabin passengers,
including Eye-witness. Then the *Sarah*
hoisted in her boats, and shaped her course
for Flores, showing a light in her mizzen
cross-trees as a guide to the *Grimshaw*
through the darkness.

All Sunday the 18th, the two vessels
continued on their course, but they could
not communicate with each other. The
weather was too wild. To the sufferers

on board the *Grimshaw*, Saturday, Sunday and Monday must have been an endless ab'yss of misery, deep opening into a still lower deep. The terrible wallowing roll of the vessel one-third full of water, the heavy swing to port and starboard, the painfully slow recovery went on without cessation, and threatened to rack the masts clean out of her. The wonder is that she did not turn turtle or be thrown helplessly on her beam-ends. Thanks to her strong construction, she kept afloat, and staggered on to eastward in the *Sarah's* wake. Sleep, food, drink, rest were strangers to the *Grimshaw;* exhaustion, hunger, thirst, fear possessed her. But weakened as they were by want of food and ceaseless labor, young Hoxie and his faithful handful stuck to their task. They could not get sail enough on their ship to keep up with the *Sarah*, and on Sunday afternoon they lost sight of her altogether. That night the *Sarah* lay-to and kept a lantern burning in the rigging. On Monday morning, she sighted the *Grimshaw* nine miles away on the lee bow. By ten o'clock the *Sarah* had come up with her, and swept by within hail, telling her to follow. Piteous cries of

'Water! Water!' rose from the deck of the emigrant ship, but nothing could be done for them. The weather was still too wild to permit of sending off boats, and the *Sarah's* supply of water was scanty enough. The *Grimshaw* wallowed along in her wake as best she could, under fore, and main topsails, foresail and fore-topmast staysail. To and fro swayed the masts, for all were loose in their steps. The mainmast could be plainly seen swaying several feet from side to side, as the ship rolled and plunged through the stormy sea; but still it stood. From the fore topgallant-yard ribbons of the lost sail streamed in the gale. In such plight, the *Grimshaw* staggered along eastward after her faithful consort, in the direction of the Azores.

Monday passed in the same way, and Monday night. On the Tuesday morning, the weather was still too wild to permit transhipping the remainder of the emigrants, but Captain Cook was at last able to render some assistance. He sent off a boat in charge of the *Sarah's* second mate with seven fresh hands, nameless sailor-men who volunteered to go. Quickly they spread more sail on the *Grimshaw*. With her mainsail, main topgallant and mizzen topsails set, she made better way; and the rocking masts still stood up. Back came the *Sarah's* boat, with five spent sailors of the *Grimshaw's* crew. They brought sad news. Twenty of the emigrants had died on the Sunday, and sixteen more on Monday night. That very morning four more had collapsed from hunger, thirst and sheer exhaustion. In the ceaseless rolling, the poor creatures must have been flung in heaps from one side to the other and half drowned in the scuppers. There must have been sore bruises if not broken bones. And when the breath left the tortured bodies, the corpses would roll helplessly among the equally impotent living. And this hell lasted at least three nights and three days. Some emigrants had broken into the doctor's stores and drunk what they found there, laudanum probably amongst other drugs, and so passed away in a numbing stupor. Others were maddened, and tried to kill young Hoxie. The tale is at its darkest, when hope dawns. About eleven o'clock, Flores was descried as a dim cloud on the skyline forty miles to the eastward. Nine hours later the two vessels were safely under its lee.

It was now eight o'clock of a pitch black November night. Transferring passengers by night is no easy task, but the state of the *Grimshaw* and the weather conditions decided Captain Cook to attempt it, at all risks. At once the work began, and here again James Coward, first mate, comes to the fore. There would be strong arms at the oars of the boats, ropes over the side and lanterns showing on the bulwarks of both vessels. To and fro between the stationary ships, the *Sarah's* boats plied, for nine hours. Though all were faint with thirst and semi-starvation, though some of the women and children were in a dying condition, not one was lost. Between eight o'clock one night and five o'clock next morning, the work was done. One more dangerous job remained to do. The unguided *Grimshaw* must not be left adrift, a menace to navigation. Coward and his men made one last trip to the abandoned ship. They boarded her once more, and, at the risk of their lives, knocked out the wedges from the heavy iron bars which secured the tarpaulins

over the hatches. As soon as the smoth-
ered fire tasted air, the whole ship was one
flame; but Coward and his boat's crew got
away safely. In the black morning hour,
the blazing ship lit up the ocean. From the
Sarah's deck, Eye-witness observed that
the *Grimshaw* began to burn from the
stern forward. With the removal of the
hatches, the flames shot up the mizzen-
mast; and it was the first to go over the
side. The rickety main-mast crashed after
it, before fire reached the topgallant sail.
The last of the ill-starred *Grimshaw* was a
dismasted flaming hulk drifting away two
miles south-west of Flores.

The survivors were safe on board a
staunch vessel in charge of as able a master
mariner as ever trod a quarter-deck. A
haven of refuge was not far away. But
their troubles were not yet at an end. The
Sarah was still smaller than the *Grimshaw*,
measuring only 857 tons, absolutely without accommodations of any kind, except
for her crew. All the rescued had to
shake down on the open deck, with no shelter but the sky. Besides, no ordinary merchantman could possibly be prepared to
feed a sudden addition of more than three

hundred and fifty passengers. The *Sarah* had only six small casks of water and provisions for one week. It was at once necessary to put every one on short allowance; the ration was half a pint of water per day, and half a biscuit morning and evening, just enough to keep body and soul together. Those who had been crying out for water, when the *Sarah* passed on Monday, could have had scant relief. It must have been during the confusion of the first day that an incident occurred, which was related to the present writer by Captain Cook's grand-daughter. How discipline vanished on board the *Grimshaw* has already been told. Most of the crew stuck by the ship and backed their officers like sailors, but some behaved badly. It must have been some of these 'packet rats' of whom the tale is told. Cook was walking the quarter-deck in the dusk, with his big brass spy-glass under his arm, concerned with the navigation of the *Sarah*. Below on the main deck, the emigrants were getting their half-pint of water per head doled out to them, when the captain heard a woman screeching. A single glance told him what was wrong. Four or five 'packet rats' were trying to rob a woman of her allowance of water. He made one spring into the knot of struggling figures, and laid out the ruffians on the deck with flail-like blows of his telescope. About the same time, he found that a priest had turned a woman out of her stateroom and taken possession of it himself. Cook forgot the respect due to the cloth, and 'gave him a beating,' and reinstated the lawful occupant. If conjecture be admitted where there is no positive statement, this 'woman' was probably the 'old lady' cabin passenger in the *Grimshaw* and the stateroom was Captain Cook's own quarters. Nova Scotia skippers were famous (and notorious) for being able to command their own ships; and after these incidents, discipline prevailed on board the *Sarah*.

On the morning of Thursday, November 22nd, which is St. Cecilia's Day, eight corpses were dropped over the side of the rescue ship into the sea. Two women and six children had reached the *Sarah* and safety, only to die. Eight fewer persons however must have given little more room on deck. One hundred of the original number, who had started from Liverpool a month before, had perished. The remnant had saved their lives, and that was all they had saved. Some had not tasted water since the fatal Sunday when the fire was discovered. Their sufferings were extreme. No strong imagination is needed to picture their condition. Fortunately, the weather was not cold, owing to the nearness of the Gulf Stream. Had it been cold, says Eye-witness with conviction, many more must have perished.

About noon the wind died away, but later it came on again, and the overloaded *Sarah* headed for Fayal. She overshot her mark in the night, and when Friday morning broke, she was fifteen miles to leeward of it. The wind was dead against her, and all that day and the following night, she was slowly beating up to the island. It was not until the noon of Saturday, November 24th that she found anchorage in the roadstead of Horta, the port of Fayal. Her supplies, such as they were, had almost run out. Only two hundredweight of biscuit and two small casks of water remained for the needs of more than three hundred and fifty persons.

The *Sarah* rode safe in port, with her

18

rescued on board; and it might have been thought that at last, their troubles were at an end. But a new difficulty emerged. After defeating storm and fire, Captain Cook encountered a fresh antagonist,— human stupidity, against which, says the poet, the gods themselves fight in vain. In the struggle, he nearly lost his life, his ship and all on board. When the port authorities came off to the *Sarah*, they informed Captain Cook that he must remain where he was, in quarantine, for five days. Reason they would not listen to. The special circumstances were not considered. Port law was port law. Every ship entering Horta must spend so many days in quarantine, and that was the end of it. So the *Sarah* remained in her first berth, held there by her anchors, and even more firmly by Portuguese red-tape. Efficient aid was promptly given by the British and American consuls. The first sent off necessities, bread and water; the second, the welcome luxuries of oranges and wine.

Sunday the 25th was a busy day for all on board the *Sarah*. She was worked a little farther into the harbour, but even this second berth was by no means safe. All day long, her boats plied between the ship and the shore, ferrying one hundred passengers to the lazaretto, and bringing off barrels of biscuit and casks of water. In the evening, a small barque, the *Clara P. Bell* sailed for New York. Her captain offered a passage to eight of the cabin passengers, but only two were allowed to go. The other accommodations were taken up by Captain and Mrs. Hoxie, the child, young Hoxie, who certainly deserved a rest, the second mate, the steward and the stewardess. Before leaving, Hoxie chartered the *Sarah* to carry the surviving passengers of the *Grimshaw* to New York. He also wrote a letter to the agents, Caleb Grimshaw & Co. in Liverpool apprising them of the loss of his ship. It is not an ingenuous letter. It tells nothing of his abdication, or the splendid service rendered by his son. It is larded with pious phrases such as 'The Lord be praised,' which would appeal to a firm of Quakers. Its only good feature is enthusiasm for Captain Cook. 'God bless him,' 'with a heart as big as Nelson's monument,' are two of Hoxie's references to him. So he departed in the *Clara P. Bell*, and now he is out of the saga.

'Wrecked in port,' is not the empty phrase of a poet. It describes the fate of many a ship. It was almost the fate of the *Sarah* in the port of Fayal. The condition of the poor, starving, exhausted emigrants shelterless on her deck moved Captain Cook to 'repeated complaints.' At last, they had their effect and the wooden-headed Customs-house officials consented that quarantine should end on Tuesday morning. It might have been several hours too late. Tuesday morning might never have dawned for any one on board the rescue ship. On the Monday, nearly one hundred more emigrants were taken ashore to the lazaretto; but more than that number still remained on board. The wind began to blow hard from the south-west, and made the position of the *Sarah* dangerous. Foreseeing trouble, Captain Cook sent ashore for an extra anchor and chain-cable. It was sweated on board, and let go. The wind increased to a living gale, and a third anchor was dropped. As night came on, the gale grew ever more violent, and all three anchors began to drag. Foot by foot, and yard by yard, the *Sarah* was forced back and back, before the tempest, nearer and nearer to the dreadful lee shore. Few situations, short of absolute wreck, render the courage and skill of the seaman so futile as when his ship is dragging her anchors. He is at the end of his devices. There is nothing for him to do but wait, and watch the danger becoming more imminent. Pitched and tossed and flung to and fro by the waves, the bulk of the *Sarah* tugged and jerked against the anchor-flukes in the bottom of the roadstead. At ten o'clock the strain proved too much for the best chain-cable; somewhere in its length, the stout links snapped; and the safety of the ship hung by the two cables that remained. For another hour and a half, the agony of apprehension continued, and in that time the *Sarah* had dragged five hundred yards nearer the line of breakers crashing on the shore and gleaming white through the blackness of the night. They were almost under the stern. Death was staring them in the face. Again Eyewitness precises the situation:

'We thought it hard to perish thus, having escaped destruction so lately, to be sacrificed to those absurd quarantine laws; and harder still that Captain Cook should die a victim to his humanity in saving our lives.'

What Cook himself expected is plain from his action. He left the deck and went below into the cabin to tell the ladies to dress themselves. He thought the *Sarah* would b'e on the rocks in the next few minutes. And then, in their extremity, —there was a lull; the vessel ceased to drag; the furious wind chopped round to the west; and they were saved. How narrowly they escaped was evident next morning, when the *Sarah* got her anchors up and moved farther into the harbour. On one, both flukes had been broken off. At the critical moment when the wind changed, the *Sarah* was held back from destruction by a single anchor. Such are the chances of life and death at sea.

The morning brought the end of quarantine, and security. The remaining passengers were put on shore, where they received every kindness and attention from the British Consul. From November 27th until December 14th food and water for 350 passengers were taken on board and some sort of rude accommodations arranged for them b'etween decks. The only incident recorded during the voyage to New York was two births. Two expectant mothers survived that fortnight of hunger, thirst, terror and pain in the *Grimshaw* to bring forth living children. The voyage to New York lasted thirty days. On January 14, 1850, the *Sarah* reached port. Probably she took her place among the prows which thrust their bow-sprits far over South Street, as in Bennett's famous picture. Dickens was impressed by this long vista of bristling spars.

The news of Cook's exploit preceded his arrival, and he received a royal welcome. He was lodged in the Astor House. A committee of the leading business men was formed to do him honor—'to mark their appreciation of his courage, gallantry and devotion.' On January 17th he was called before the assembled merchants in the old Exchange in Wall Street to receive a resolution of thanks and welcome. It lauds his 'humane and intrepid conduct' and repeats a phrase of Captain Hoxie's letter about his heart being 'as big as Nelson's monument.'

Cook was visibly affected by such testimonies of regard, and replied in halting, commonplace sentences, still more eloquent than the most fluent Ciceronian periods:—

'You make me feel proud.—You make me think—I have done a great deal—when I have done nothing—that was but my duty—and that my Maker did not require at my hands. I cannot give expression to my feelings at present—I am not in the habit of speaking in public. I feel most grateful for your kindness—and—I shall not soon forget it.'

There is contemporary evidence as to the appearance and bearing of this typical Nova Scotia sea-captain. The *Tribune* found him 'exceedingly prepossessing. In height, he appears to be over six feet, is finely formed, erect, manly and dignified. He has the ruddy, English countenance and an open, pleasant set of features.' The *Herald* report is not so specific. It calls him 'a fine looking fellow. Just such a man as would do a good action for its own sake.'

Plainly the hero looked the part.

The enthusiasm of the New York merchants did not evaporate in meetings and laudatory resolutions. With true American generosity, they raised a purse

278

for him of eight thousand dollars. Of this
sum, $5,000 went to Captain Cook himself,
and he distributed three thousand dollars
amongst the crew; $700 to the first mate,
Thomas Coward, $125 to each seaman, and
$100 to each ordinary seaman and boy.

Nor was this all. New York itself, the
Mayor and Corporation took official action.
On Thursday, January 24th, at two o'clock,
there was a crowded meeting in the Governor's Room in the City Hall. Along with
a most flattering resolution, beginning 'Resolved, That said David Cook is eminently
entitled to the gratitude of the civilised
world,' the Mayor presented the master
mariner out of Yarmouth with an illuminated address and the freedom of the
city in a gold snuff-box. Captain Cook was
then brought before the assembly. He was
received with hearty cheers. There was a
rush to shake hands with him. The police
from two wards, 'with their staves of office,'
were needed to preserve order. It was in
fact another 'scene of enthusiasm.' The
ladies in an adjoining room were favored
with a sight (of the hero) 'without being
crushed or jostled by the other sex.' This
must have been when the New York

ladies kissed him. The address, a triumph of Isaac Bragg's calligraphy, in the frame by Verrocchio, which cost $30, and the snuff-box are preserved by Captain Cook's descendants in Yarmouth.

On the twentieth of June, 1850, the Senate in which sat Web'ster and Calhoun, voted a gold medal to Captain David Cook; but the House of Representatives rejected the resolution. He did not therefore go without such a reward; for Lloyds presented him with their beautiful silver medal, *Ob Civos Servatos*, designed by Wyon the Royal Academician. It represents Leucothoe giving Ulysses the magic veil which keeps him safe. The reverse shows the oak-leaf garland the Romans awarded to a soldier for saving the life of a comrade. It looks as if there were little exaggeration in that phrase about 'the gratitude of the civilised world.'

Nor did Yarmouth fail to do honor to the hero. As soon as he returned from New York, there was a crowded meeting in the old Court House in Main Street. The High Sheriff presided, and Captain Cook was presented with an address signed by two hundred and thirty-five leading citizens. Many laudatory speeches were made, and then the audience dispersed, and the sailor went back to sea.

'The Thunderer' printed the narrative of Eyewitness on Christmas Day, 1849, and, in a leading article, criticised severely the *Grimshaw's* agents and Captain Hoxie. Grimshaw & Co. attempted a reply but with the usual result to those who venture to argue with a newspaper.

In 1864, Captain Cook was master and part owner of a small barque of 280 tons, built at Clementsport, and named for his eldest daughter Louisa. On June 21, 1871, the *Louisa Cook* sailed from Shields for Philadelphia with a general cargo. It was her last voyage. On September 2nd, she was spoken in lat. 42, long. 65, and was not again heard of. Her epitaph is a laconic entry in Murray Lawson's tragic list of the six hundred Yarmouth County vessels lost between 1777 and 1875.

His eldest daughter has sunny memories of her childhood home, of romps, and games of hide-and-seek through the house with her tall good-natured father, whose word still was law, when he said 'No!' She remembers his habit of walking in the garden, a child holding each hand, while he talked to himself about his day's business. 'Another remembrance was prayers in the morning before breakfast. We could offer no excuse. We were expected to be there neat and tidy, chairs placed in a half circle in our old dining-room, and all listening quietly as my father read the chapter from the Bible; then prayers; afterward a cheerful breakfast with a full table as we were a large family.'

In the old grave yard at Chebogue sleeps many a Yarmouth sailor, but many another rests in the ocean depths. No stone marks the grave of David Cook, but if ever a cenotaph is raised in his memory, it should bear the words he must have known, 'He saved others—'

The Saga of
'Rudder' Churchill

The Saga of 'Rudder' Churchill

N the great days of sail, all the counties of Nova Scotia built wooden ships, but Yarmouth, county and shire-town, stood apart in a class by themselves. Hants might run neck and neck in tonnage, and, using Georgia pine, build admittedly better ships; it might plume itself on constructing the *W. D. Lawrence,* the biggest ship ever built in Nova Scotia; there might be seventeen captains of clan MacKenzie at one time sailing out of Pictou; but nothing ever shook the primacy of Yarmouth as the most maritime county of a maritime province. Between this county and all the others, there was a cleavage. Thirty-five Nova Scotia vessels might be lying together in Antwerp docks, but the Yarmouth skippers kept themselves to themselves. Meeting other captains from the province in the street, they would pass the time of day, but their intercourse went no further. Bright, hospitable Yarmouth town is built on shipping, and *Ab Urbe Condita,* Yarmouth families have followed the sea. From generation to generation, Lovitts, Canns and Killams, Hatfields, Cooks and Churchills have commanded ships with varying fortunes in every ocean. The historic shallop *Pompey* of twenty-five tons, which brought the first settlers to the county in 1761, became the fruitful mother of whole fleets, of every rig and every size, until Yarmouth could boast the largest *per capita* tonnage of any port in the world.

Perhaps the reason for Yarmouth's pride in her ships and sailor-men, and why her master mariners were inclined to bear themselves with a difference may appear from this true tale of the ship *Research* and her commander, 'Rudder' Churchill.

The *Research* was a large, full-rigged ship of 1459 tons burden, built in Yarmouth, in 1861, by Thomas Killam, a well-known merchant of that town. On November 10th, 1866, she sailed from Queb'ec deeply laden with ton-timber consigned to William Lindsay & Co. of Glasgow. Those were the days of rafts. Huge, picturesque, floating islands of wood with sails and oars, with shanties on them and fires burning were water-borne down the St. Lawrence to Quebec. Here they were broken up, and the square 'sticks,' fifty or sixty feet long, were loaded through the bow-ports of the timber droghers for the United Kingdom. The coves of Quebec were full of these vessels, three hundred at a time, painted frigate fashion, with black, dummy ports, on a broad white streak. The *Research* was in this trade. Beside the timber in her hold, she carried a deck-load of deals, packed and lashed and wedged together into an immoveable mass. It was very late in the season for such a voyage.

Her captain was George Churchill of Yarmouth, aged twenty-nine. His photograph shows a bearded, gentle, almost dreamy face, but there was nothing vague about his seamanship. And his resolution was iron. He was known as 'Tear' Churchill, but how he acquired the violent by-name is not clear. He was a navigator of much experience, well reputed for having extricated his ship from dangerous situations, and for once having saved it from destruction by fire. The first mate was his nephew, Aaron Flint Churchill, a young giant of sixteen with more than his share of the family's good looks. He had already been two years at sea, and he was second in command by virtue of his ability, and not by any Board of Trade certificate. Flint is a Yarmouth family name, but it betokens the quality of his will. If he had never done so before, he was to prove his manhood in this voyage. George Marshall, also a Yarmouth man, was boatswain, and every inch a sailor. As always, the officers were the spear-head of the less resolute crew.

More than a fortnight was spent in getting down the river, but, by the night of November 26th, the *Research* was clear of the dangerous straits of Belle Isle, and fairly out on the Atlantic. That night, the wind almost died away, and the barometer fell to 28°, a most ominous hint of trouble to come. Every precaution was taken. Sail was reduced at once to close-reefed topsails. The *Research* carried double topsails, Forbes's patent, which means that the second sail from the deck on each mast was in two parts, with two yards. Closereefing meant only the lower half showing. The yards were braced round inboard, to present the least resistance to the wind. With all made snug, as the sailors say, the *Research*, stripped like an athlete, awaited the onslaught of the storm. All night the uncanny lull continued, but with the morning the tempest broke. Out of the northwest it came, a typical winter storm from the frozen Pole, with a fury and a violence which Elizabethan seamen would term outrageous. It smote the *Research* like the hammer of Thor. It ripped the three topsails from the yards and flung them on the waves, leaving only streamers of canvas whipping from the bolt-ropes. Worse was to follow. A tremendous sea struck the rudder and broke the rudder-stock a little below the 'casing,' or opening in the stern through which the stock passes, to connect with the tiller and the wheel. The same deadly blow snapped the half-inch links of the rudder-chains. The latter led from a large ring-bolt on the back of the rudder to the rail, or the quarter. They might be called emergency, or safety, chains, because if the stock were broken, the ship could still be steered by means of tackles shackled on to them. Now both stock and chains were broken. The vessel was definitely out of control. The gale, which began with such force, continued, with one brief lull, for a whole month, growing ever worse and worse.

Short of total dismasting, the plight of the *Research* could hardly be more desperate. She could carry no sail; her rudder was useless, and worse than useless, for it was pounding heavily against the rudder-post. The rudder-post is not, as its name might imply, a single piece of wood, but a complex of strong timbers heavily backed by other timbers framed together with all the shipwright's art. It holds the afterpart of a vessel together, as the keystone holds the arch. Injury to it may mean a fatal leak. Without a sail, without a rudder, the *Research* drove helplessly before the winter storm. A rudderless ship in a storm is a proverb for impotence and disaster.

The rudder is the most important part of a ship. St. James, with his experience of navigation on Galilee, was impressed with the contrast between the great ship and the small rudder which yet turned the ship about whithersoever the governor listed. But if the rudder is hopelessly disabled like the rudder of the *Research*, what then? Something must be done, and George Churchill was not the man to fold his hands and resign himself to calamity. Attempts were made to pass a hawser over the stern, around the wildly flinging rudder, and so hobble it. The expedient served only for a short time. The hawser chafed through, and the pounding rudder began to break up. How to fetter the massive piece of mechanism and prevent further damage was the problem. If tackles could be affixed to the big ring-bolt on the back of the rudder, it could be controlled, and the ship steered from the deck. But the rudder of a loaded vessel is practically all under water, and the *Research* was wallowing in mountainous seas. The first thing to do was to lighten the ship aft and so bring the ring-bolt to the surface. The careful stowage of the deck-load had to be undone, and the bright, fresh-cut deals thrown overboard. It was a long and dangerous job, but it was done. The *Research* was down by the head, with the stern considerably higher than the bow. And all the time, the gale blew harder, and the billows swept the deck, and the spray froze where it fell.

The next morning was November 28th. The stern of the *Research* was now sufficiently elevated to permit of tackles being fastened to the ring-bolt on the back of the rudder. There was but one way to fasten them. A man must go down into the water and affix them. As the stern projected far over the rudder, as the rudder itself was constantly battered to and fro by the fierce waves, the difficulties of such a task must be plain to the meanest capacity. And who was to do the job? It is in such emergencies that the first mate comes to the fore. On that bitter winter morning, Aaron Churchill stripped to the buff and went over the side 'in a bowline.'

'He wouldn't be much colder without his clothes,' said the Port Warden reflectively, when he heard of the incident.

Going over the side in a bowline, even in bad weather is no uncommon feat for a sailor. When the staunch but mishandled *Osberga* began to leak through her bow-ports, which should never have been cut in her, Captain David Douglas went down in a bowline to repair the damage. He was often six feet under water. Charles Doty, first mate of the *Native*, was four hours in the water passing a chain lashing round her rudder which had come adrift; but he spent three months in a New York hospital afterwards. Captain Borden Marsh did the same thing during his fortnight of starvation on board the brigantine *Cleo*. The Port Warden himself learned what the pressure of the water can be, as he dangled in a bowline. But the circumstances attending Aaron Churchill's feat are, one may say, unique.

Bowline is a sea term, with several meanings. It is, in the first place, the safest knot a sailor makes. It is simple, quickly tied, and it will not slip. Bowline also means a rope with a loop in it fastened with this safe knot. The sailor sits in this loop, and thus can be swayed up to the masthead, if necessary. As the Port Warden demonstrated with the domestic clothes-line, what Aaron Churchill sat in, was a double bowline. One loop went round the thighs; the second went under one armpit, and over the opposite shoulder. Each loop draws against the other, and the knot is just over the heart, thus leaving both hands free. In such a harness of three-inch rope was the first mate of the *Research* lowered over the side and into water with a temperature somewhere near freezing-point. With one hand he held the tackle, a hooked block, or pulley, through which ropes ran. The hook must be slipped through the ring, when opportunity offered. This was a one hand job. Churchill needed his other hand to save himself from b'eing battered to death against the side, or the overhang, of the vessel. On the deck above him, men paid out the line, or stood by to haul, and watched and lifted when the waves swept over the man below. It is safe to infer that the master and the boatswain managed the rope on which hung the fate of the ship.

'Impossible!' said the Port Warden, in the voice he used to hail the masthead with, when he came to this part of the story. 'He may have gone over in a bow-line, but never in that weather. Why, he would have been smashed up against the counter, and killed. He might have gone down perpendicular, but never under the stern.'

The Port Warden was very decided and emphatic. But the evidence is irrefragable. Here are the contemporary accounts in *The Times* and *The Glasgow Daily Herald;* here are the entries in Captain Churchill's own hand-writing preserved by his niece Margery in Yarmouth. Family tradition has handed down precise detail which could not have been invented. Years afterwards, when he was a rich man, Aaron Churchill had a picture painted. It represents a full-rigged ship in a violent storm, and a man hanging by a line under the stern. A reproduction of it states specifically that the man in the bowline is Aaron Churchill. The fact is well attested, but the scepticism of a practical sailor like the Port Warden shows that this deed is unique, even in the marvellous chronicles of death-defying first mates.

That bitter November day, Aaron Churchill needed all his wonderful strength and vitality. In years a boy, he was already a man grown, half an inch over six feet, perfectly proportioned, with muscles of iron. Freezing water, icy wind, drowning, broken bones, being battered to death against the overhanging counter were some of the dangers he had to face. Besides, the huge, heavy rudder was never at rest, but beating continually against the rudder-post with terrifying violence. Frozen, blinded, half-strangled, Churchill must watch for the favorable second when the ring-bolt was near enough for him to slip the hook of the tackle into it. Victor Hugo imagined a fight between a man and an inanimate object, which seemed endowed with demoniac life, the gunner and the carronade adrift between decks in the *Claymore;* but under the stern of the *Research*, a mother-naked man waged a real battle against the brute force of a huge piece of mechanism, which, as it flung incalculably to and fro, threatened every instant to maim or kill him. That day Aaron Churchill was fighting not for his own life, but for the lives of all on board. Impossible as it seems, it is yet a fact that he did what he went down to do. The Churchills have the name of being 'dogged.' After an hour and a half of incredible labor, he succeeded in hooking one tackle into the ring-bolt. He was hauled up on board insensible and laid out on the deck to recover. Half a pint of brandy was poured down his throat. Slowly he revived, slowly his strength returned; and then,—he went down over the other side of the ship with the second tackle.

This time he was down for an hour and three-quarters by the clock, one hundred and five minutes of freezing, of strangulation, of desperate exertion, but, somehow or other, he managed to fasten the second tackle in the ring. One more typical first mate's job was done. The dangerous rudder was securely hobbled; the *Research* was once more under control, and could be steered by the ancient device of pulling and hauling on the tackles. Aaron Churchill was dragged back to the deck more dead than alive, or as the unemotional *Times* report has it, 'when taken on board was insensible, but recovered.'

With the help of the sails the vessel was kept on her course until the 29th, that is until the next day. By the will of the master, and not by the will of the storm, the bowsprit of the *Research* pointed eastward to Greenock, her port of destination. But wind and wave are pitiless antagonists. The results so painfully obtained by Aaron Churchill at the risk of his life, hardly lasted twenty-four hours. On the 29th what was left of the rudder was torn from the pintles and swept away. Even a damaged rudder was better than none, and now the *Research* had not even a fragment of hers left.

Such accidents were not uncommon in the old days of sail. Captain Samuels of the flash packet *Dreadnaught* of the Black Ball line lost his rudder, off the Banks of Newfoundland. He took in his head-sails, backed his yards, and navigated his famous vessel six hundred miles, stern first, to the Azores. With a broken rudder-stock, two days out of Philadelphia, Farquhar of the *Cumberland* got tackles on his rudder, and, steering 'pully-haul', brought his ship across the Atlantic. The resourceful sailor had other expedients in such emergencies. He could tow a cask or a spar astern, or he could even construct a rudder. Archie Campbell of the *Piscataqua* and his mate Joe Blois built and shipped a jury rudder, when the original was lost. They saved ship and cargo; and the underwriters of Havre gave the captain a gold watch. In the examinations for their certificates, would-be mates and masters were often asked how to rig a jury rudder. It was naturally considered a most important point.

A rudder must be strong. As built in the shipyard, its nucleus, or core, was the 'stock,' a single timber of seasoned white oak, long enough to reach from the keel up through the opening in the deck, the whole depth of the vessel. To this central timber were firmly bolted a massive fore-piece and a back-piece, so fashioned that the three were as if hewn out of the trunk of a single tree. It was attached to the stern-post by three right-angled hooks, or 'pintles' fitting into corresponding 'gudgeons,' or rings. Though so huge and massive, a rudder had to be built scientifically, so that a line drawn through the three 'pintles' would run through the axis of the 'stock.' To build such a rudder on board and 'hang' it in a winter gale so that the 'stock' would come through the 'casing' and the 'pintles' drop accurately into the 'gudgeons' was manifestly impossible. Rigging a 'jury' rudder was a different matter.

A 'jury' rudder was often made in two pieces, consisting of the stock, and the rudder itself. The latter was simply an oblong mass of heavy planking bolted together lengthwise and crosswise, as firm as the ship-carpenter's art could make it. No attempt was made to give it the correct, original, oar-like shape. This rude substitute was hinged to the stock by stout rope lashings, or, better still, by chain 'grummets,' running round the 'stock' and through auger-holes in the top and bottom of the rudder. The whole, heavy, clumsy contrivance with all its trailing ropes attached had to be hoisted out-board, lowered over the stern, and the stock drawn up through the 'casing.' Through the top and bottom of the rudder ran stout ropes, or chains, if available, for they do not stretch, which were carried far forward on each side of the ship, and hauled taut. These would draw the rudder hard against the rudder-stock and hold both firmly against the rudder-post. To make the mechanics of the device plain to the landsman's comprehension, it might be said that this home-made rudder was tied to the stern by four strings. By means of two other 'strings' attached to the outer edge of the rudder by a looped rope called a 'bridle,' and also carried far forward, the rudder was pulled this way or that, at the word of command.

To construct even such a rudder involved much hard labor with edge-tools, adjusting, calculating, measuring, shaping, sawing, hammering, boring, joining, on the reeling deck of the laboring *Research*. Aaron Churchill gets the credit of having done most of the actual work. The deck-load of deals was not all started overboard; enough remained to supply materials for more than one or two jury rudders. For two days and two nights, the big timber-ship drove impotently before the storm, while officers and men toiled at the indispensable steering-gear, or snatched a mouthful of food, or an hour's sleep. On the morning of December 2nd, the jury rudder was completed. It was being lowered over the stern, when a wicked cross-sea caught it, and snapped the hawser like a thread. Away floated the rudder. All this painful labor was useless.

This sudden failure might have daunted any but a Nova Scotian ship-master; but George Churchill was as fertile in devices as that other sailor-man of ancient song,

the many-counselled Ulysses. He made a
steering-oar. The wheel-house had been
wrecked by the hammering seas. Churchill
tore down what remained of it, in order
to have a clear field for his next experi-
ment. The *Research* carried spare spars,
roughed out 'in four,' or 'in eight,' lashed
to the bulwark stanchions. Churchill took
a spare top-mast about sixty feet long, and
to one end he bolted a huge square of the
deck-load deals. It must have looked like
a wooden spade for Gargantua. This would
be secured to the rail by strong lashings,
which still would permit of its being moved
to and fro. Other stout ropes would hold
the inboard end in place. Like the jury
rudder, this enormous steering oar would
be moved to port or starboard by means
of lines fastened to the 'spade' itself, and
carried far forward. So it was made. Apparently it was ready for use the very next
day, December 3rd; and hoisted into position. But it was a failure. It did not af-
fect the vessel's way. She would not 'pay
off' before the wind. By lightening the
Research aft, in order to get at the ring-
bolt in the rudder, the stern was lifted high
out of the water. It was therefore neces-

sary to jettison part of the deck-load forward in order to restore her trim. So it was done.

On Decemb'er 4th, the huge steering-oar was again hoisted over the stern; but it could not be sunk deep enough in the water to influence the way of the *Research*; she was a big ship. It had to be taken on board and weighted, perhaps with 'thirteen fathoms of chain,' or even an anchor. Next day, it was again hoisted out; the necessary leverage was gained, but the weight was too much for the spar. The handle of the 'spade' was fractured by the strain, about ten feet from the upper end. In spite of the break, these unconquerable sailormen got their vessel under control, and, by the aid of their damaged rudder, and also by deft management of such scanty canvas as they dared to set in that living gale, they sent the *Research* storming along eastward, and ever eastward. When they could take advantage of it, the tempest's fury was driving them towards their destination. The directing will of the master was guiding his ship to her predetermined goal.

Painfully the damaged steering-oar was

hauled on board. Once more there was heavy carpenter-and-joiner work on the iced and reeling deck, where no landsman could even keep his footing. From the 6th to the 9th of December, the vessel drove ahead without steering-gear of any kind. By December 9th the oar was spliced and repaired; but in attempting to hoist it out, the ropes gave way and let the huge concern down on the deck, where it had to be secured and lashed fast. Amongst other minor jobs of this voyage was bending fresh convas. Those three lost topsails had to be replaced. The Port Warden says that it is not necessary to send down the yards; sails properly rolled and stoppered, he avers, can be bent on, in a gale of wind.

Nature is pitiless. The furious storm not only continued but grew more and more malignant, as if the elemental rage were bent solely on defeating these toiling pigmies, and overwhelming the cockleshell in which they trusted. Moving hills of water broke over the helpless *Research*, smashing in the forward deck-house where the crew lived and wrecking the provision-locker. Soon they were on short allowance; and before the voyage ended their food ran out altogether.

No stauncher vessels ever swam than the best products of Nova Scotia shipyards, but no fabric of man's handiwork could endure for weeks such battering from wind and wave as befell the *Research* without showing the effects. She began to leak. The oakum in the two big bow-ports worked out and the sea came in. A timber-laden vessel cannot sink, but she can become water-logged, a helpless, unnavigable hulk below the level of the waves. To avoid this calamity for days and weeks, day and night, spell and spell about, officers and men labored at the wheel-pumps amidships, two at the handles and others tailing on to the ropes. Constant pumping kept the water down, but could not prevent it from coming in.

Still in spite of wet, and cold, and exposure and the heart-breaking labor at the pumps, the men of the *Research* built a third rudder, and, during a lull on the morning of December 14th, they got it 'shipped,' that is, tied on behind, like jury-rudder Number One. For a whole day, this clumsy contrivance functioned, and the vessel answered to her helm; but on the 15th, the violent seas smashed the stock, and the rudder was useless.

Evidently the stock of this latest failure was jammed in the 'casing,' or 'trunk;' and it was with no little trouble that Churchill and his men worried the massive wooden post out of the hole. For nearly another week, they could do nothing but hold on, and work the pumps. All that time, the *Research* was wallowing in the trough and swept by 'high, irregular seas' raised by hurricane weather. On this account, the narrative continues, apologetically, it was 'impossible to begin work earlier' than December 21st. To make matters worse, one pump was now disabled. But on the twenty-first, a new rudder, Number Four, was begun. When it was finished is not recorded; but by January 2nd, 1867, it was got into its place, 'after much labor.' This rudder held, but it was not powerful enough to control the way of the vessel. 'It was necessary to put an additional rudder over the stern, like a steering-oar, worked with tackles from in-board.' It is difficult to keep tally of Churchill's inventions, but this makes Rudder Number Five.

Navigating a leaking ship in hurricane weather, with two jury-rudders, the men pulling and hauling on two sets of tackles at the word of command must have presented difficulties, but Churchill the indomitable met them, overcame them, and kept his vessel on her course until January 5th, when 'the stock of the other was carried away and the rudder lost.' And now Rudder Number Four is out of the saga.

Somehow or other, about the turn of the year, the leaking, rudderless, crippled *Research* had traversed the Western Ocean from the Straits of Belle Isle to a position within fifty miles of Tory Island at the north of Ireland. Then she was about one hundred miles, as the gull flies, from her port of destination. And then,—the gale came round to eastward, dead in her teeth. 'A series of hurricanes and heavy seas' drove her back and back, south and west, out into the Atlantic, eighteen hundred miles out of her course.

Away from the north of Ireland to the neighborhood of the Azores, the *Research* was scourged and driven. Still more harm was done her by the hammering seas. They 'swept the decks, stove in the hatches

and carried away bulwarks.' Let the lay-
man, who has noted the massive strength
of hatches and bulwarks estimate the
weight of water which would smash them
down from above, or tear them from the
ship's solid frame. With Scottish reserve,
The Glasgow Daily Herald remarks:
'The officers and men were frequently
greatly exhausted, and upon several occa-
sions the crew desired the captain and officers to give up the ship.'

'Don't give up the ship!' is a famous
watchword, and the principle involved is
held as firmly in the British mercantile
marine as in the Royal Navy. No bull-dog
captain, who nailed his flag to the mast,
and fought till not a stick would stand, ever
displayed more resolution and tenacity of
purpose than this quiet-faced, plain, merchant skipper out of Yarmouth. George
Churchill had not the slightest intention of
giving up his ship, even when he had still
stronger inducements to abandon her.
Such a case as the *Thomas E. Kenny*
abandoned at sea is still remembered to
the disgrace of the captain. The skipper
of the *Noel* left her on the rocks, after
thirty-six hours labor, but she was after-

wards salvaged, and it broke his heart. Backed by his splendid nephew, and cheery, courageous, determined George Marshall, the captain of the *Research* persuaded his crew to remain at their duty, when their situation seemed desperate and their labour all in vain.

On January 10th, in spite of the ocean's spite, Churchill prepared to send down his main-yard to form the stock of a new rudder. That he was ready to sacrifice this important spar shows the extremity of the *Research*.

'Why didn't he use his cro' jack yard?' the Port Warden asked.

Without the main-yard, the operation of 'heaving-to,' or stopping the ship's progress in the sea, would be well-nigh impossible. But the presumption is that Churchill knew what he was about. Three days later, the sixth rudder was constructed, and after 'several mishaps' was got into place. Rudder Number Six was not carried away by the turbulent seas; it lasted until January 25th, but it was not large enough to control the big ship effectively. Still it was better than nothing, and, with its aid, Churchill the unconquerable, navigated the *Research* towards Greenock.

Ever since the northwest blizzard struck her on the morning of November 27th, the big timber-ship had been, as if abandoned by God to the |will of the storm, solitary under wintry skies, on the waste of waters; but now she was nearing the great traffic lanes between the old world and the new. Help was coming to her. On January 16th, she spoke the ship *Empress Eugenie*, Collins, master, homeward bound from San Francisco. Across the stormy sea, whipping signal flags told her story. Both ships hove-to; and the boat of the *Research* rowed off for provisions. After such a long voyage, the *Empress Eugenie* could not have had much beef and biscuit to spare, but she did what she could to help a sister in distress. The very next day, the steamer *Palmyra*, Watson, master, also on her way to Liverpool from New York hove in sight and stopped to assist the crippled but unbeaten *Research*. From both these vessels, Churchill received 'great kindness and friendly offers of aid.' From both he accepted sorely needed supplies, but he refused to be taken off. An abandoned ship may mean a total wreck; but it may also mean big salvage, almost the value of ship and cargo. Pride, interest, duty forbade him to take the easy way out of his difficulties; and he stuck to his ship.

Besides the *Empress Eugenie* and the *Palmyra*, the *Research* received help from a third un-named vessel. That the three friendly, helpful captains offered to take Churchill, and his crew off his battered, leaking vessel with her crazy steering gear shows what they thought of her condition. In a raging storm, they had stopped to speak a wreck, which would never make port. At least the odds were decidedly against it. So the three ships went their several ways. When she reached Liverpool, the *Palmyra* thoughtfully telegraphed Lindsay & Co. that she had spoken the *Research* and supplied her with provisions. This was welcome news to the consignees, for they had long ago given her up for lost, and were even then arranging for the insurance on the ship and cargo. It was, of course, during these three sea-parleys with their would-be rescuers that the crew wanted to abandon the ship. Starving and exhausted as they were, with little prospect of saving their lives, no one can blame the over-tasked foremast lads, or withhold admiration from the iron-willed triumvirate of officers who refused to admit defeat.

Rudder Number Six could not be dislodged, but it was not working well. Churchill built a seventh on an improved plan. It was begun on January 25th, and, 'after several ineffectual and heart-breaking efforts,' was shipped two days later. The last line was hardly hauled taut, the rudder-stock was hardly home in the rudder-casing, when the stock broke and left it disabled. So Rudder Number Seven is out of the saga.

By this time, the *Research* had clawed back from the neighborhood of the Azores to the south of Ireland. The unbreakable resolution of the master was overcoming every difficulty. Churchill built another rudder, and on the first day of February, about 185 miles south-west of Cape Clear, it was shipped without mishap. Practice makes perfect. These Nova Scotia handymen had learned from their failures and experiments. Seven is a complete, a mystical number. Poseidon was apparently satisfied with the sevenfold sacrifice. For Rudder Number Eight was a success. With this triumph of perseverance, the luck of the *Research* changed; the wind became favorable, and urged her up the Irish Channel. At Ailsa Craig, she fell in with a tug, and accepted a tow. It was no disgrace. After a voyage of eighty-eight days, under her own sail, with the aid of her eight improvised rudders, the *Research* had made port. She was hauled to the Wooden Wharf at the Tail of the Bank. Next day the *Glasgow Daily Herald* printed a brief item of shipping news:—

'Greenock: Arrived, February 5th, *Research*, Churchill, from Quebec with timber.'

That is all the landsmen would learn of the long duel between the spirit of man and the rage of ocean. And the man won.

At the Wooden Wharf, the *Research* was an 'object of considerable curiosity.' Well might she be! Very different she appeared from the trim portrait of her that hung in the owner's office in Yarmouth with every sail set and her flags flying. To the landsman's eye, she must have seemed a wreck. Main yard, forward deck-house, wheel-house were gone; great ragged gaps showed in her bulwarks; her deck was cumbered with strange gear; and astern was her home-made rudder, but the costly hull was sound, and the precious cargo in the hold was intact. The insurance money would cover all repairs.

This tale has a happy ending. To the three unconquerable Nova Scotians came tangible rewards for their conduct as well as gratifying and well-earned words of praise. On March 10th there was a notable gathering of gentlemen in the Underwriters' Room of the Glasgow Exchange. They were convened for the purpose of presenting Captain Churchill and his two officers with various testimonials 'in approbation of their conduct while in charge of their vessel on her voyage from Quebec to the Clyde.' Of the Glasgow Underwriters,— douce, home-keeping bodies,—not one was interested personally in the ship or cargo, to the extent of a penny-piece; but they knew how to admire pluck and perseverance. They put their hands in their pockets and b'ought a silver salver for Captain Churchill, engraved in plain terms with the record of his great exploit. This piece of plate is a treasured heirloom in the possession of his eldest daughter near Yarmouth. The Chairman of Lloyds sent him a letter, commending his 'indomitable perseverance.' The Union Marine Insurance Company presented him with a gold watch and chain, and a purse of sixty sovereigns. Pious Mr. Euing, senior member of the Underwriters made the presentations, and expressed the hope that these brave men would always be protected by Him who ruled the winds and 'Who will bring all those who put their trust in Him, to a haven of enduring rest.' And the Glasgow Underwriters clapped their hands.

In his manly, seamanlike reply, Captain Churchill made them laugh by saying that 'If shipmasters did not act as they should, underwriters required to increase the premiums, so that it came out of the owner's pockets in the end.' Of course, he also said what every sailor would say: 'he had done no more than was required of him.'

Churchill's achievement is unique in the annals of the sea; and, to the end of his days, he was famous among his brother captains as 'Rudder' Churchill. This honorable appellation was known even to the school-children of Yarmouth. His pretty eldest daughter was teased, when her school-mates cast up the nick-name to her, not knowing in her innocence that it was a greater honour and more dearly won than many a patent of nobility.

Nor did the services of the mate and the 'invaluable' boatswain go unrewarded. To each was given a silver chronometer, watch and gold albert chain by the Underwriters on the cargo, and a sextant in a case from the Union Marine Insurance Company.

Not many years after this memorable voyage, Aaron Churchill quitted the sea, and, like so many other able Canadians, found opportunity waiting for him in the United States. He went into the stevedore business, invented several labor-saving devices, founded the Churchill line of steamers out of Savannah, and made his fortune. It is told that behind his office he had a small room fitted up as a gymnasium to preserve his great strength. He never forgot his native Yarmouth. On the shores of Lake Darling, he built himself a summer pleasance, which he named 'The Anchorage.' During the Great War, he helped with sailor-like generosity to swell the county's subscriptions to patriotic funds and Victory Loans. When the United States entered the war, he put the Churchill fleet at the disposal of the government; and he gave his employees liberal inducements to serve their country. In a complimentary address, the Georgians likened him to General Oglethorpe, the founder of the colony. He lived out the allotted span and died in his bed; but he never forgot that bitter winter day under the counter of the laboring *Research*.

The *Lennie* Mutiny

The 'Lennie' Mutiny

'ISCIPLINE' on the lips of Nova Scotia ship-masters is accented on the second syllable. With them, both the word and what the word represents had a quality all their own. The question Jervis once put to the wavering captain of a mutinous crew, 'Do you mean to say that you cannot *command* His Majesty's Ship *Essex*?' never applied to the master mariners of Nova Scotia. They were kings of the quarter-deck. Undoubtedly they had a hard name for their iron rule. No Liverpool magistrate, it is said, would decide a case in their favor; but the New York merchants preferred them above all others for their proved ability to deliver their cargoes. 'You would see sixty odd sail of us lying together in New York,' said the Port Warden, 'Seven or eight of the Carmichael fleet by themselves.'

Those old-time skippers had many

dangers to face besides the everlasting hazards of wind and wave. Yellow Jack was always a menace in the tropics. 'I buried fifteen men at Aspinwall,' said Captain Fred Ladd, casually, in discussing the failure of de Lesseps. Once when Mac-Arthur of the *Milton* reached Rio, he found the crew of every ship in harbor stricken with the deadly fever. Till very lately, pirates were to be encountered in the West Indies. Freights were paid in sacks full of Spanish dollars, in defence of which Nova Scotia captains have undergone half-hanging, or had their throats cut. Nor was life on board one's own ship always safe. Crews were an uncertain quantity. No one could tell what foreigners were thinking of, or what they would do. They had a curious way of looking down at you, when they went aloft. Ship-masters slept with loaded revolvers under their pillows. Every now and then there were murderous outbreaks. 'Bully' Howard aided by his daughter, quelled a mutiny in a South American port, but he was badly wounded in so doing. When the furious negroes tried to knife his mate, Borden Marsh, single-handed, backed them into the fo'c'sle. The story of the racket in the *Sherwood* has not been fully told; but the crew never had the bandages off their heads till they reached Antwerp, and then they jumped ashore, as the ship was moving through the dock-gates. The crew had numbers on their side; but the afterguard had organization. Sometimes victory did not lie with the officers.

On October 23, 1875, the full-rigged ship *Lennie* lay in Antwerp, awaiting a crew. She was a vessel of 984 tons register, built in Belliveau's Cove in 1871, and owned by William W. Lovitt of Yarmouth. She was going out in ballast to New York for orders. On board were the officers, the young captain, Stanley Hatfield aged twenty-five, of Riverdale, Yarmouth County, the first mate Joseph Wortley, an Irishman and the second mate Richard Macdonald. The steward was a Belgian, Constant Van Hoydonck, who had sailed in the *Lennie* for two years; he was much attached to Captain Hatfield and was the same age. He had as assistant a boy named Henri Trousselot from Rotterdam. About eleven o'clock, Long the London runner brought on board a crew of eleven men, who had just crossed the Channel in the *Dolphin*.

They were destined to return to London
before very long, but not as they expected.
The steward told the captain of their arrival. Four Greeks, tall, heavy, black-
haired, black-bearded men, three Turks, an
Austrian, an Italian, a Dane naturally
called Peter Petersen, and a degenerate
Englishman, one Charlie Renken made up
as mixed a crew as ever berthed in a Nova
Scotian fo'c'sle. The ceremony of signing
the ship's articles took place in the presence of the British consul. One of the
foreigners, the so-called Austrian, Giovanni
Canesso, was something of a linguist,
speaking English, German and Italian. He
was there and then rated as boatswain with
increased pay, and berthed aft. Captain
Hatfield went ashore with his trusty
steward, and Trousselot served the men a
plentiful dinner at noon. The same day,
the *Lennie* made her departure for Sandy
Hook.

Real names are not often heard in the
fo'c'sle. Cargalis was known as 'French
Peter.' He was a jail-bird, and had acquired
French, while serving an eight year sentence in the prison at Marseilles. Caladis
was 'Big Harry,' Kaida the Turk was

called 'Lips,' Moras became 'Johnnie Moore;' Angelos, another Turk answered to 'Little George,' Canesso, the boatswain, was christened 'Johnny Green.' One foreigner in a crew can be managed; two or three together almost certainly meant trouble; but a fo'c'sle full of Levantines was a serious problem. Some difficulty would be experienced in licking such a mixed crew into shape. It may not have been true that the first job of a Nova Scotia first mate on the first day out was to thrash every man before the mast, but his duty was to maintain discipline, with the accent on the penult, and he did not use merely moral suasion. Understanding little English, it was hard for such a crew to learn to pull together. Their lubberliness would naturally irritate a smart Yarmouth captain, and the Hatfields had the name of 'overbearing;' but, according to the steward, Stanley Hatfield did not abuse his men. No questions were asked about the mate's conduct, and Van Hoydonck is eloquently silent on that head. There was no real trouble for the first week out. Some of the men were great smokers, and ran out of tobacco. They applied to the captain for some; but he had only enough for himself.

By October 31st, the *Lennie* was in lat. 49° 4" N. long. 6° 35" W. about 180 miles from Falmouth, working down Channel against head winds. Wortley, the first mate, had the middle watch, from midnight until four. Then Hatfield turned out of his bunk, and came out in the dark, in his wooden clogs, and took command. The captain's watch had been called up; all hands and both mates were on deck. Hatfield gave two or three orders for putting the ship about, and the clumsy Levantines fouled the braces. The ensuing confusion is clearly due not to accident, but to premeditated design. At twenty minutes past four, Van Hoydonck in his berth under the quarter-deck heard the shouted orders, and high words. Then Hatfield sang out.

'That's always the case. You're a parcel of soldiers, not sailors.'

This speech as reported may have been Bowdlerized. As a deep-sea reproof it seems mild, especially as addressed to foreigners, and compared with what an accomplished reprover like 'Tiger' Cann could say. But it was the match to the train of gunpowder. Hatfield may have struck the nearest man, and that man may have been Big Harry. Certain it is that Big Harry drew his knife with deadly swiftness, stabbed Hatfield in the face, and instantly followed up with the ghastly, disabling belly-slash. His sureness of aim in the dark implies practice. Next year, another Greek almost disembowelled poor Captain Best of the barque *Caswell* with the same blow. Another Greek tried it with Worthington of the *Nice*, but the second-mate was quicker with a belaying pin; and there was one Greek less in the world. This peculiar stab seems especially Greek. Hatfield was desperately wounded, but he defended himself with his fists, the natural weapons of the Nova Scotia sailorman. Had he brought with him on deck only one of the two revolvers at that very moment lying under his pillow, this story might have been different. Big Harry stabbed again. The whole crew came rushing aft; heavy feet pounded on the deck; French Peter joined in the life and death struggle and drove his knife twice into Hatfield's neck. He fell to the deck dead, or dying. In his berth a few inches below, Van Hoydonck heard a horrid, choking, gurgling sound. The second mate Macdonald rushed to his captain's aid, but too late. Seeing the two fleshed murderers b'ent on killing him also, he ran to the boatswain Green, flung his arms round him, and begged for his life. Green disengaged himself, and pushed Macdonald away, and Big Harry, with two fierce thrusts, felled him to the deck. Wortley, the first mate, raced up the fore-rigging. He did not get far, and he could hardly have hoped to escape. The crew followed fiercely the chief object of their hatred. Cacaris a Turk, known as Joe the Cook, shot at him from below, Lips swarmed up the rigging above the doomed man and fired at that vantage. Van Hoydonck heard five pistol shots. Some took effect; Wortley fell from the ratlines to the deck. Knife in hand, French Peter leaped on him, and nearly severed his head from his body.

In a few fierce minutes that dark October morning, three strong men were laid bleeding corpses on the *Lennie's* deck. The grimy fo'c'sle plot was completely successful. Everything points to concerted action. The mutineers were masters of the ship.

Van Hoydonck made a brave effort to

aid his captain. He took the two revolvers from under the pillow in the captain's bunk and went to the companion-way. He found Lips and Big Harry guarding it. He could not force it open. The other exit was likewise held against him. He got on the cabin table and tried to climb out by the sky-light; but Renken, who was at the wheel, saw him and shouted a warning to the crew. Some ran aft. Van Hoydonck saw Renken by the binnacle light, realized how impossible it was to do anything, and gave up trying to break out of the cabin. He must have expected speedy death. The guarding of the cabin-doors proves a plot and the plotters' belief that the steward would stand by his captain.

Then, after the turmoil on deck, the shouted orders, the outcries, stamping, running feet, noises of deadly scuffles, sharp barks of the pistol, silence fell on the *Lennie*. A brooding hush pervaded the unguided ship like the irresolute pause in *Othello,* when Desdemona's struggles have ceased.

Then again, there was activity on deck. The murderers dragged the three still warm corpses amidships. To the captain's body, they fastened a pump, and to the first mate's, some mooring chain, which was attached to the second mate's body by a ring-bolt. Thus united in their sea-burial as in their death, the three were heaved overboard. But afterwards the sea gave up the dead. In similar fashion did the Greek mutineers of the *Caswell* dispose of their officers. There are hints and whispers of incredible outrages on the bodies and stories told in fo'c'sle's and sailors' taverns; for the rage of the Greeks was not slaked by the mere death of their enemies. Even more gruesome tales are told of the *Caswell*.

Down below in the big cabin, Van Hoydonck and Trousselot awaited they knew not what. They must have felt that murder most foul had been committed; they must have feared that their turn would come next. Time passed slowly in the apprehension of death. Van Hoydonck had the captain's revolvers in his pockets. No doubt he would have used them at need; but, even so, his chances against the eleven would have been slight. At ten minutes to six, the red-handed mutineers came down into the cabin, with Green, the boatswain at their head. The parley that followed was curiously commonplace. Said Green,

'Well, steward, we have finished now. We have done the job.'

'What have you finished?'

'We have finished the captain, mate and second mate, and thrown them overboard.'

'You can navigate?'

'Yes, a little.'

'We have made up our minds to go to Greece. If you want to save your life, you had better take charge of the ship. If you take us to Gibraltar, we will find Greece. Johnny Moore and I have a rich uncle. He owns many ships. We will scuttle this vessel and take to the boats. My uncle will buy everything, and he will give you a berth in one of his ships. You will have your share with the rest of us,—the charts, sextant, everything.'

Then, for the benefit of the big, black-bearded ruffians filling the cabin, Green translated into Greek. They assented.

'All right, steward!'

Van Hoydonck then asked where the bodies were. Green replied,

'Oh, they are all right. They are overboard.'

Then all went up on deck, and Van Hoydonck took command of the masterless *Lennie*. In the dim November dawning, he saw a sight, which could not have done much to steady his nerves. The deck was a wet carmine. Blood covered the captain's walk on the starboard side. There lay his cap, jacket and clogs soaked in blood. There was blood by the cabin-door, blood on the planking close by the main mast, and blood on the fore-rigging about eight feet from the deck, where the mutineers' bullets had found Wortley. The three officers were not to be seen.

Knowledge is power. Now Van Hoydonck's knowledge of navigation saved his life. These ignorant foremast hands could not read a chart, or lay a course, or take the sun. They did not even know in which direction Gibraltar and Greece lay. Left to themselves, they must have soon blundered into trouble. The ship would have run away with them. Being asked to take command was a reprieve for Van Hoydonck. Henceforth, his one idea was to bring the murderers to justice. Acting as captain, he re-established the ship routine; he divided the crew into two watches, taking one himself and assigning the other to Green. He tried to keep a log, which may be an incriminating document. He wrote the entries on a slate; but every morning Petersen came down into the cabin and rubbed them out. This Belgian steward was a man of no mean capacity; he made no mistakes in his navigation.

That morning of All Souls Day, 1875 on board the *Lennie* must have stretched out interminably. Some of the men set to work to swab' the blood-soaked deck, foreshrouds and ratlines. Others undertook to disguise the ship, as futile an expedient as trying to conceal the identity of the Great Pyramid. One man painted out the name on the bows; another, the name and port of registry on the stern. Still others whittled *Lennie* off the boats. The *Saladin* murderers did the same thing, not realizing that a ship without a name is an object of suspicion on every ocean. If spoken, her rig, size, position would be promptly logged and reported. The Man in the Iron Mask might as well expect to walk down Broadway and escape notice. There is no hiding on the high seas.

When these jobs were done, the mutineers came down into the cabin for breakfast. Then they proceeded to plunder. Johnny Moore took possession of the keys and ransacked the various rooms and boxes. Big Harry dressed in the captain's clothes, and slept in the captain's bed.

Next morning, November 2nd, there was a scene on the poop. Van Hoydonck relied too much on the sailors' ignorance and laid a course for Lundy's Island. Renken took the wheel and recognized his marks. He cried, in alarm.

'Steward you are not going to Greece, but to some part of the Channel. I can see it.'

'Mind your own business,' Van Hoydonck retorted. 'If you don't keep quiet, I'll blow your brains out.'

But Renken was not intimidated. He left the wheel and ran forward, shouting,

'That steward is going to sell us. He's not going to Greece. He's going to the Channel.'

All hands hurried aft. Big Harry asked,

'Where are you going?'

'I'm going to Greece, and if you let me alone, I'll take you there.'

Van Hoydonck was a man of character

and of no little force. His words and bearing imposed on the crew, and he was not molested further at that time. Seeing, however that it was impossible to make an English port, he altered the course of the *Lennie* at 11.30 just before his watch ended, and steered south and east. The new course was in the general direction of Gibraltar, but it was also in the direction of France. Next day, he sighted a schooner but French Peter made him bear away from her. If too close, the strange sail might spy the damning erasures at the *Lennie's* bows or stern.

Steering for Brest, Van Hoydonck brought the *Lennie* into the bay of Sables d'Olonne near the Ile de Ré, on November 4th. Big Harry was suspicious. There was land all round. At various points, light-houses showed their twinkling lamps. He wanted to know what Van Hoydonck was doing there. The steward replied stiffly that he knew what he was about. He proposed to anchor, and give all hands a night's rest. But French Peter still objected, and threatened to cut his throat if he betrayed them. So the *Lennie* was hove-to until the morning.

No doubt Van Hoydonck was disappointed at this check, but he did not betray himself or give way to despair. Nor was he at the end of his resources. He wrote a note in French and English for Trousselot to copy. The English version ran:

Please send as soon as possible plenty police, tug-boat and men, because sailors have murdered the captain, mate and second mate. We left Antwerp for New York, Oct. 23; the mutiny took place on the 31st. If the police keep them below so that we can save our lives. The name of the ship *Lennie*, three-masted, Capt. Hatfield.

(Signed)

Constant Van Hoydonck,
Steward.

Trousselot made half a dozen copies. Van Hoydonck put them into bottles, which he corked, and unobserved by any of the crew, dropped overboard. His hope was, of course, that they would drift ashore and bring a rescue. Three bottles were actually picked up, and one of Trousselot's notes was afterwards produced in evidence.

That same night, Van Hoydonck had a conversation with Joe the Cook, as they kept watch together. Joe reassured him.

'Don't you be afraid! They won't do you any wrong so long as you see us safe to Greece. We have killed three. We do not want to kill any more. I am afraid they will kill the boy lest he split on them and tell the tale.'

Of course, Van Hoydonck promised that Trousselot would hold his tongue.

At another time, French Peter and Big Harry spoke to him about the danger of the boy 'splitting,' and again Van Hoydonck promised for him.

At five o'clock next morning, in spite of the head wind, he was forced by the suspicious Greeks, to take the *Lennie* to sea again. French Peter warned him.

'I'll have to do with you, as I did with the rest, if you sell us.'

Van Hoydonck took a bold stand; he refused to navigate the ship any longer. Petersen was put in his place; but he soon showed himself to be hopelessly incompetent. For two days, the *Lennie* wandered aimlessly on the high seas. On the evening of the 6th, Big Harry came down into the cabin, and asked Van Hoydonck to take charge again. He agreed to do so, but on his own conditions. One was that if he found a port, he would go in and anchor. Accordingly, he worked the *Lennie* back to the Roads of La Flotte by the evening of November 7th, and anchored, paying out plenty of chain, so that it would take a long time to weigh. He told the Greeks that they were at Cadiz. That night he locked Trousselot in his cabin, so that no one could see what he was doing, and had him make twenty copies of the informing note. These copies he put into as many bottles, and, unperceived, committed them to the sea. Unperceived also he managed in the dark to hoist the ensign, union down.

The stupidity of trying to conceal the *Lennie's* identity by obliterating the name was now become apparent. On Saturday, November 6th, Pilot Réde watching for a job far at sea, observed a vessel seemingly out of her course. Without boarding her, he followed her into the Roads and showed her a safe anchorage. On the Monday morning, he noted the strange sail was flying the universal signal of distress; and he put off to inquire the reason. At first, the weather was too bad for him to come close and he signalled his question; later, he manoeuvred within hail. Now, for the first time, some one on board noticed the signal of distress, and French Peter hauled it down, saying it was a 'police flag.' He forced the steward below and assumed the rôle of captain. He told the French pilot that the chronometer had run down, and that they were riding there until they should have a fair wind. Réde could see for himself that the ship's name had recently been painted out, and he could get no information about her nationality. He returned in the afternoon with a letter written in Italian. This time he came on board with the letter. French Peter told him to bring one in English or French. The look of the ship and the demeanor of the crew were so suspicious that as soon as the pilot got ashore he reported to the Prefect of Marine.

These inquisitive attentions were too much for the murderers' nerves. They resolved to escape from the ship. On the next morning, November 9th, they asked Van Hoydonck what country this was. He told them it was a republic, a free country, with no police,—anything to get rid of them.

Six of them decided to go off in the long-boat, French Peter, Big Harry, Joe the Cook, Lips, Nicholas and Little George. All but Little George had a bundle of the murdered men's clothing and effects. They wanted money, and tried to get some from Van Hoydonck. He had none. They searched one another for coin, stripping Lips to the skin, to see if he had any concealed about him. The long-boat would hold only six men; the other five planned to quit the ship the following night. Before leaving, the six exacted a promise from Van Hoydonck that he would remain on board for a fortnight, but he noted the direction in which they rowed, and he made up his mind to go ashore the next day and inform the authorities. So the six rowed away from the ship, with their plunder and their vain hope of evading Nemesis. One curious thing was packed in Big Harry's little bundle, the photograph of Miss Belle Lent of Tusket. He took the picture out of the captain's album; but left the album itself on board. Why should a murderer want the picture of a pretty Nova Scotian girl?

The six mutineers did not get very far.

At the first inn, they told the landlady that they were shipwrecked sailors of the Greek brigantine *St. George,* loaded with wheat, from Constantinople for Havre, which had foundered at sea. It was not a likely story. The telegraph was put in operation, the falsity of their tale was revealed, and the six were arrested. They stuck to their story but, under pressure, Angelos, the boy told the truth.

On the morning of November 10th, the gunboat *Tirailleur* came alongside the *Lennie.* The captain hailed Van Hoydonck and told him to send off his boat. There was trouble on board. The steward had to drive the men into the boat at the point of the pistol. Renken was especially mutinous. When Van Hoydonck told his story, the French captain immediately sent him ashore to communicate with the police. Later, he gave him ten armed sailors to arrest the remaining mutineers. With them in custody, Van Hoydonck must have breathed freely for the first time in ten days.

Six weeks were spent in legal proceedings before the French courts decided that they had no jurisdiction in such a case, and

the whole crew were taken back to London
for trial. They were first tried before Sir
Thomas Henry; but Mr. Justice Brett,
afterwards Lord Esher, presided at the end.
During the course of the trial, Van Hoydonck was sent over to France, in order
to view the ghastly remains of the tragedy.
Three trunkless heads, and one naked headless body had been cast up by the sea upon
the French coast near where the mutineers
landed. The fishermen who found the
heads, buried them, and could not find the
place again amid the shifting sand. The
headless body of rather a tall man had
sixteen incised wounds in it, but it was so
decomposed that Van Hoydonck could not
identify it. This may have been the body
of Stanley Hatfield. The four guiltiest
mutineers, French Peter, Big Harry, Joe
the Cook and Lips were sentenced to death,
and duly hanged by the neck until they were
dead, according to British law. The rest
were discharged.

Through the fidelity of Van Hoydonck,
the murderers had been brought to justice,
and the vessel saved for the owners. He
was the most important witness; his testimony sent the murderers to the gallows.

After putting on the black cap and condemning them to death, Judge Brett directed the faithful steward to stand forward in the court, and pronounced a memorable eulogy upon him. He praised him for his 'courage, fortitude and dexterity' in bringing about the arrest of 'these wicked men,' and for protecting the defenceless boy Trousselot, at the risk of his own life. 'Every honour is due to you,' said the representative of British Themis. Judge Brett expressed the wish that he could award Van Hoydonck some decoration, but, as that was not in his power, he directed that £50 be paid to this faithful steward for his 'honourable and courageous conduct.' It must have been a dramatic scene, the guilty punished, and, in their sight, the virtuous publicly rewarded, in that dingy London court-room. No legal authority can call to mind a parallel.

This was not Van Hoydonck's only reward. In consequence of Judge Brett's eulogy, the aristocratic Order of St. John of Jerusalem awarded him their silver medal, and their bronze medal to Trousselot. Van Hoydonck was afterwards a uniformed gate-man at the Antwerp docks and well known to Nova Scotia skippers.

After the affair of the *Lennie* and the mutiny on board the *Caswell* off Antifogasta, Jan. 4, 1876, Greeks were not employed in the British merchant marine for many a year. Captain James Wright of Digby sailed from Cork with a Greek crew immediately after the trial of the *Caswell* mutineers; he confessed to feeling 'skittish' about them, but they gave no trouble. The *Lennie* mutiny has features in common with the *Saladin* murders, even to the time, the plundering, the mutual distrust, the disguising the ship, and the stupidity of the criminals. The leading motive of the Levantine cut-throats in the *Lennie* is not quite clear. Was it revenge for ill treatment? Was it hope of enriching themselves with the plunder of the ship? Was it a mixture of the two?

Nearly fifty years afterwards, in the golden haze of a rare September day, when every branch was scarlet with autumn and the yellow dahlias were a-flame about the old Hatfield homestead, Ned Hatfield told a sympathetic visitor the story of his brother Stanley's end. Below, the winding Chebogue glittered like silver. Over all

344

was the peace of the mellowing year, a perfect contrast to the deed of blood that dark October morning on board the *Lennie*. Tears were in Ned Hatfield's eyes, and his fine old face was troubled, as he bade the visitor good-bye.

'Stanley was all right,' he said. 'He never bore a grudge. We never knew just why they did it.'

.   .   .   .

Qualia multa mari nautae patiuntur in alto.

WARWICK
BROS. &
RUTTER
LIMITED
TORONTO
PRINTERS & BOOKBINDERS